Essays in Evangelical Social Ethics

Essays in Evangelical Social Ethics

Edited by
David F. Wright
Senior Lecturer in Ecclesiastical History,
New College, University of Edinburgh

EXETER
THE PATERNOSTER PRESS

1978.

ISBN:
Casebound: 0 85364 288 5
Study Edition: 0 85364 290 7

AUSTRALIA
Bookhouse Australia Ltd.,
3-7 Richmond Road, Homebush West, N.S.W. 2140

SOUTH AFRICA
Oxford University Press,
P.O. Box 1141,
Cape Town

British Library Cataloguing in Publication Data

National Evangelical Conference on Social Ethics,
Hoddesdon, 1978
Essays in Evangelical Social Ethics
1. Christian ethics - Congresses
2. Social ethics - Congresses
3. Evangelicalism - Congresses
I. Title   II. Wright, David F.
241   BJ1189

ISBN 0-85364-288-5
ISBN 0-85364-290-7 Pbk

Typeset in 11 point Times by Photoprint, Paignton, Devon, and printed and bound in Great Britain by Butler & Tanner Ltd., Frome, Somerset, for The Paternoster Press Ltd., Paternoster House, 3 Mount Radford Crescent, Exeter, Devon.

CONTENTS

Introduction

HIGH LEIGH CONFERENCE CENTRE AT HODDESDON IN Hertfordshire was the venue for five days in September 1978 of the National Evangelical Conference on Social Ethics. Over a hundred invited members assembled under the chairmanship of John Stott. They were drawn preponderantly from the younger ranks of Evangelicals and ranged from academics, schoolteachers, ministers and doctors to business men, people in the arts and the media, M.P.'s, youth leaders and social workers. A small Scots contingent and at least one Irishman gave a limited British dimension to the predominantly English gathering, and a handful of overseas representatives contributed at times an international perspective.

The plenary addresses, published in this book very much as they were delivered, formed the backbone of the Conference. Members had received synopses of these papers in advance, and should have been well prepared to discuss them at the Conference in small groups. In the event, feedback from the groups provided scant guidelines for the speakers in revising their papers for publication. The other main activity of the Conference were the workshops on topics that included Northern Ireland, trade unions, medical ethics, social pressures and the family, and the just war and armaments.

The secretary of the organizing committee was Pat Dearnley, a vicar in North London and a former Director of the Shaftesbury Project. The full administrative resources of the Project under its present Director, John Gladwin, were marshalled in support of the Conference. Since much of the

credit for the Conference's achievements belongs to the growing stature of the Project, a few words about it will not be out
of place.

The Shaftesbury Project was founded in 1969 to promote a
biblically-based approach to areas of social concern. It draws
together evangelical Christians from a wide range of occupa-
tions, church allegiances and political viewpoints. Basic to
their co-operation in the Project are the twin convictions that
God's self-revelation in Christ presented in the Scriptures
must be fundamental to any attempt to relate Christian
beliefs to society, and that a full-orbed Christian discipleship
will not neglect such a responsibility. The Project is particularly keen that not only experts and leaders but also church
members in general be stimulated and equipped to be salt and
light within their social context. To this end it makes
available a steady flow of papers, news-sheets, booklets and
memoranda, mostly produced by its study groups working in
areas such as race relations, overseas development, crime and
punishment, and the role of women in society. The Project
enjoys increasing recognition as a kind of evangelical 'think-
tank' for social and political issues, and a resource centre for
churches and Christian groups and agencies to call upon.[1]

The High Leigh Conference was the first national evangelical venture into the field of social ethics to be held in
Britain. As such it reflected and endorsed the growing
acknowledgement among British Evangelicals of the biblical
imperatives of social concern and action, to which the
Lausanne Congress on World Evangelization gave international expression in 1974.[2] The relative newness of this commitment among Evangelicals may be set alongside what
Ronald Preston has recently identified as 'a certain loss of
impetus in Christian social ethics' in Britain since the early
1940's.[3] As far as Evangelicals were concerned, little or no
impetus was discernible in the first half of the century.

---

1. Further details of the Shaftesbury Project may be had from the Project office,
8 Oxford Street, Nottingham, NG1 5BH.
2. The Congress papers were published as *Let the Earth Hear His Voice*, ed. J. D.
Douglas (Minneapolis, 1975). See especially 'Evangelism and Man's Search for
Freedom. Justice and Fulfillment' by Samuel Escobar (pp. 303-326), and 'Christian
Personal and Social Ethics in Relation to Racism, Poverty, War and Other Problems' by Carl Henry (pp. 1163-1182), but many other contributions are relevant to
social ethics. Klaus Bockmuehl has subjected the Lausanne statements to a cautious
biblical critique in *Evangelicals and Social Ethics* (Exeter, 1979).
3. R. H. Preston, 'Whither Social Ethics?', *The Modern Churchman* 21 (1978),
pp. 81-95, at p. 81.

The roots of this neglect of social ethics are many and various. Some of them are unearthed in the chapters of this book. Professor Preston rightly detects in evangelical Protestantism 'an excessively individualist outlook which has led it to suppose that problems of collective ethics can be solved provided we have individually consecrated persons facing them'.[4] It is surely no accident that fresh awareness of the social implications of the gospel should follow in the train of a widespread rediscovery of the significance of the church in evangelical teaching. At the same time the kingdom, or better, rule or reign, of God has had to be rescued from its almost total entanglement with evangelical 'futurology', and hailed as begun on earth in the works of Jesus — a reign the signs of whose inauguration among men included the feeding of the hungry, the healing of the sick and the ingathering of the flotsam and jetsam of human society. It would be difficult to refute the charge that the evangelical quest for heaven had too often been attended by a devaluation of the welfare and just ordering of man's earthly life, a failure to accord proper weight in our thinking and priorities to the world of God's creation. The dominant sentiment was well expressed by the Reith Lecturer, Edward Norman: 'the wise aspirant to eternity will recognize no hope of a better social order'.[5] Although the importance of social involvement has been regularly acknowledged, it has somehow rarely seemed important enough to engage more than marginal commitment. Evangelical ethics have for the most part been content to be personal rather than social.[6]

It is against this background of large-scale evangelical neglect of social action and reform (except vicariously in the reverence paid to our forebears, especially of Shaftesbury's era), that these papers must be judged. They are concerned with what John Gladwin calls 'the shaping of the mind', rather than with determining attitudes or promulgating programmes on particular issues. It is at the level of the evangelical mind that the battle for social ethics will have to be won. If evangelical groups and churches are to embark on

4. *Ibid.* p. 90.
5. E. R. Norman, *Christianity and the World Order* (Oxford, 1979), p. 79. See the responses to these Lectures in *Christian Faith and Political Hopes,* ed. Haddon Willmer, London, 1979. Norman is no Evangelical, and Evangelicals will be wise not to embrace him as an unexpected ally. Not least should this be evident from his treatment of the persecution of Christians in the U.S.S.R. on pp. 33ff.
6. See, for example, the inadequate treatment in *A Guide to Christian Reading,* ed. A. F. Walls, London, 1952 (revised 1961).

Christian discipleship in this area they will need to hear a
summons that is Bible-based and gospel-based as well as
society-based.

Evangelicals will justifiably want to be assured of the
biblical grounds for socio-political obligations and activity.
Establishing such grounds is an objective to which each of the
essays in this collection makes its distinctive contribution.[7]
Howard Marshall carefully plots the path in general terms,
concluding that 'the task of the moralist is to extrapolate
from Scripture to the particular ethical exhortations appropriate in different situations'. The God-given natural order as
a basis for ethical directions is examined by Oliver
O'Donovan, and compared with the ethical import of historical revelation and eschatology. He helpfully exposes the
different 'cash-value' of the two approaches, the naturalist
and the historicist, in relation to differing cultural and social
situations. Like Oliver O'Donovan, David Lyon declines to
accept the choice between creation ethics and kingdom ethics,
but proceeds instead to present the significance of the four
pivotal 'moments' of biblical history — creation, fall,
redemption, consummation — for a Christian response to the
challenge of Marxism. It is probably true that Evangelicals
have been inclined to make too little of the Bible go too far in
this sphere. In seeking a biblical view of political responsibility, Romans 13:1-7 has been for many the one and only port
of call, while the doctrine of God's 'common grace', a doctrine with scarcely a broad biblical basis and only tenuously
rooted in Reformation theology, has had to bear ever-
increasing weight in interpreting God's involvement with the
non-Christian world of men and nature. The essays in this
volume will hopefully serve to suggest a more extensive
biblical undergirding of social ethics.

In particular, if Evangelicals, that is to say,
'gospel-people', are to make a consolidated advance on this
front, they must be clear about the *relation between the
gospel and social concern*. John Stott's discussion of this central issue in *Christian Mission in the Modern World* (London,
1975) had been an influential catalyst of evangelical thinking,
anchoring social commitment in the pattern of the Father's
sending of the Son. (Surely the miracles of Jesus are fraught
with often unexplored significance in this connexion?) No
less important has been Article 5 in the Lausanne Covenant,
which deserves to be reproduced in full:

7. See also Bockmuehl's essay referred to in n. 2 above.

We affirm that God is both the Creator and the judge of all men. We therefore should share his concern for justice and reconciliation throughout human society and for the liberation of men from every kind of oppression. Because mankind is made in the image of God, every person, regardless of race, religion, color, culture, class, sex or age, has an intrinsic dignity because of which he should be respected and served, not exploited. Here too we express penitence both for our neglect and for having sometimes regarded evangelism and social concern as mutually exclusive. Although reconciliation with man is not reconciliation with God, nor is social action evangelism, nor is political liberation salvation, nevertheless we affirm that evangelism and socio-political involvement are both part of our Christian duty. For both are necessary expressions of our doctrines of God and man, our love for our neighbour and our obedience to Jesus Christ. The message of salvation implies also a message of judgement upon every form of alienation, oppression and discrimination, and we should not be afraid to denounce evil and injustice wherever they exist. When people receive Christ they are born again into his kingdom and must seek not only to exhibit but also to spread its righteousness in the midst of an unrighteous world. The salvation we claim should be transforming us in the totality of our personal and social responsibilities. Faith without works is dead.

In these collected papers Haddon Willmer attempts to glimpse a theology of the state which is in our sense gospel-based, that is to say, determined by the God-for-others who is the man Jesus Christ. Here the state belongs not solely to the realm of common grace or a fallen humanity but embodies something of 'the "for-other" reality of the gospel'. Haddon Willmer has followed up his Conference paper with another testing exploration of 'The Politics of Forgiveness'.[8] John Gladwin was at pains in his Conference address to unfold the implications of the Christ of the gospel for human rights — both the creativity released by the yielding of rights and the foundation for respecting the integrity of the conscience of others. And several papers pinpoint the importance of the church, the community that lives by and for the gospel, as the model for the reordering of human society. David Cook suggests we should view it as a test-bed, where, in exploring, for example, masculinity and femininity, 'we can afford to make mistakes, recognising that God's grace is always sufficient'.

But if an evangelical social ethic is to be Bible-based and gospel-based, it must also be earthed in the realities of society. Here belong the essential contributions of social

8. Haddon Willmer, 'The Politics of Forgiveness', in *Third Way* 3:5 (1979).

scientists and fieldworkers, whether doctors, lawyers, parents or politicians. Here we also note the value of John Briggs's historical survey of the transition from Christendom to our contemporary pluralism — a transition which he welcomes rather than laments. In so doing he perhaps speaks for a minority among British Evangelicals, but a minority with an increasingly articulate voice, partly as a result of a small but far from token American Mennonite presence in recent years. Evangelicals who trace their lineage back to the magisterial Reformations of Luther, Zwingli, Calvin, Cranmer and Knox have too long been able to ignore the alternative witness of the Anabaptists. Their claim to be more consistently biblical than the major Reformers is a challenging one. Their present-day heirs have recovered their penchant for posing radical biblical questions in books like John Yoder's *The Politics of Jesus* (Grand Rapids, 1972) and Ronald Sider's *Rich Christians in an age of Hunger* (London, 1978).

There can be little doubt that ethics for society are much easier to fix when that society is a greater or lesser Christendom. The peculiar dilemma of British Evangelicals in the last decades of the twentieth century can be stated in some words of Ronald Preston: 'we have inherited the structures of a Christendom situation but without the reality of it, and are tempted to a nostalgia for its return'.[9] Some at the Conference were convinced that the desire to restore reality to the structures of Christendom was no nostalgia, let alone a temptation, but a viable Christian objective. The issue remains a tricky one, and the parting of evangelical ways is not far distant. Are biblical ethics (Old or New Testament?) for the whole of society or only for God's people? How far should we in practice accommodate to the political, social and legislative realities of pluralism, which are coloured in various shades of grey but rarely black or white?

In its short history Marxism has become a determinant of social reality for the world's population almost as influential as Christianity. David Lyon's searching consideration of the challenge of Marxism (now backed up by his monograph *Karl Marx: A Christian Appreciation of his Life and Thought,* Tring, Herts, 1979) could not have been omitted if we were to do any kind of justice to the contemporary scene. As an ideology Marxism is uniquely related to Christianity and remains a standing witness to the failure of Christians to give

9. *Art. cit.* p. 93.

social embodiment and expression to the loving justice of their God.

Furthermore, evangelical ethics require the input of social and economic analysis if their theological undergirding is to be not only biblical but also contemporary. Howard Marshall's paper broaches the question whether there is such a thing as progress in ethics analogous to development in doctrine. How should Evangelicals respond creatively to the gospel and its implications in order to meet the needs of today's world? The challenge is a central one for theology no less than for ethics. The story of theological development — of creeds, articles and confessions, of *Institutes of the Christian Religion, Systematic Theologies* and *Church Dogmatics* — reveals the articulation of church doctrine largely in response to heresy and schism (ecclesiastical disturbances) on the one hand and through interaction with philosophy, history and science (intellectual pressures) on the other hand. It is arguable that for the forseeable future theology will have to be done at the interface with two fronts which have come to the fore only with the twentieth century. These are presented by the vitality and resurgence of other faiths or religions and the needs of an unequal world. The former of these challenges is taxing enough, although Christian history can throw up some precedents to guide the modern theologian. (I think especially of Christianity's encounter with the distinguished tradition of Greek wisdom in the early centuries.) But never before have the clamant needs of millions of undernourished, underprivileged, oppressed people constituted a creative factor in the explication of the church's theology.

What can we, what must we say *biblically and theologically* about a world — God's world — marked by such massive inequality and injustice as ours, a world in which the dividing lines so detrimentally isolate the so-called Christian west? How must our traditional church doctrines be 'developed' in order to make Christian sense — Bible sense, gospel sense — of such masses of humanity reduced almost to sub-human existence? If theology of an earlier era dare not for its own vitality and integrity fail to confront the philosophical currents of the day, if theology 'after Auschwitz' dare not for shame ignore the Holocaust in speaking of the Jewish people, no more may evangelical theology today neglect to take account of the dominant social, economic and political realities of the world. There lies before us here an undertaking which will require constant interaction in thought and

reflexion between the biblical basis, the gospel basis and the
socio-economic-political basis for evangelical social ethics
spoken of above. These are largely uncharted waters for evangelical
mariners. Indeed, injustice will be done to these Conference
papers if they are viewed as statements of an established
evangelical consensus. Some of them display more of a tentative or adventuring quality than others. They all raise questions, some of which are appended to each chapter for group
discussion. There must surely be a place for experimental or
provisional thinking and writing, as we endeavour to move
into new territory or grapple with moral dilemmas and social
developments which our forefathers could never have fore-
seen. Evangelicals must summon the courage not merely
to respond to the pressure of changes in society, such as the
shrinking of the world to the size of a 'global village', the
ethical problems posed by technological advances and the
growing totalitarianizing of political life in west as well as
east. We must claim the freedom and confidence to map out
new paths ahead of the pack and before we have to face the
inescapable. If orthopraxis and orthodoxy are both appropriate terms in this field, then both are as much goals to work
towards as starting points to work from.[10]
    The High Leigh Conference should therefore be hailed not
as the sign of a new-found evangelical maturity but rather as
the seal on an evangelical conversion. We have not arrived
but we have reached the end of the beginning; having put our
hands to the plough we must no longer turn back. In one
respect, however, we may hope and pray to be found mature
travellers — in accepting the propriety of different routes and
stopping places on the journey. The Conference delegates
neither reached nor were programmed to reach unanimity,
whether in discussing the main addresses or in workshop
debate. Unionists and managers, capitalists and socialists,
champions of Christendom and advocates of gathered churches in secular society, conservatives and radicals — along
these and other lines divisions were unmistakable. But
Evangelicals have long learned to maintain fellowship in the
faith despite deep-seated disagreements — on baptism, the
nature of the church, the ordering of its ministry, the first
things and the last things and many others in between. The
critical factor will not be the convictions or policies that

10. With John Stott's Epilogue on 'Tasks Which Await Us' may be compared
Bockmuehl's pages on 'The Task Ahead', *op. cit.* pp. 39-43.

divide us so much as how we live and work together despite
the divide.

Another reason why Evangelicals may expect strains and
frictions in social ethics lies in the instinctive caution that has
come to characterize so many of their attitudes. Have we not
tended almost unthinkingly to appreciate peace and order in
preference to the disturbance that alone may bring forth
justice? Are we not inclined to react automatically against the
clamorous demonstration, the disruptions of the strike, the
confrontations of the hustings, without asking whether the
customary peace and quiet mask the sleep of death, the
putrefaction of stagnant waters and the suppression of ugly
injustice? How do we Christianize our instincts?

But if protest and struggle must come, the tone of evangelical involvement must be distinctive. Can we engage in the
hurly-burly of party politics without rancour? Can we chip
away at the massive blockages to social health without
fatalism? British society can rarely have been in greater need
of an injection of hopeful and charitable conviction to
counteract the acids of cynical denigration. And if more and
more Christians incarnate the biblical principle that 'a
spiritually liberated person also has a concern for *earthly*
liberation',[11] should we not look in faith for the expression of
that concern to fructify the preaching of the gospel? So may
the church of God grow and the hurt of the world of God be
healed.

---

11. Bockmuehl, *ibid.* p. 9.

Chapter One

The Natural Ethic

Oliver O'Donovan

CHAPTER ONE

The Natural Ethic

Moral Disagreements

To Begin With The Most Trivial Of Observations:
ethical judgements are controversial. Why are they so?

In the first place, controversies arise about matters of fact.
Some people think that marijuana does, and some people
think that it does not, damage the body and mind of those
who smoke it. Which of these beliefs is true will make a considerable difference to our moral judgement on the smoking
of marijuana. There is a respectable philosophical tradition
which supposes that all moral controversy is due, in the last
analysis, to the want of hard information. The utilitarians of
the nineteenth century, for example, who are enjoying something of a revival today, thought that moral judgement was
essentially a matter of accurate prediction: if one could know
exactly what consequences would follow from each of the
alternative courses of action, one would be in no doubt as to
which to follow. In such a theory there is no such thing as a
genuinely *moral* disagreement. Values as such are not up for
discussion — they are supposed to be uncontroversial, or
perhaps, more aggressively, non-negotiable. Within the community of reason, only the facts can be a matter of legitimate
doubt or dispute.

But the most profound and terrifying moral controversies
resist this kind of rationalization.

Which is why a second tradition of philosophical thought has represented moral disagreement as a function of inscrutable personal commitment. If clashes of moral conviction cannot be resolved by factual information, it appears that moral conviction is not susceptible to rational arbitration at all. There is a place for reason, of course: reason clarifies what the alternatives are, reason can tell us what will be involved if we hold to a certain judgement consistently. But when reason has fulfilled its office, we have simply to make our choice. Reason is the handmaid of personal decisions which go beyond reason; and there is no way that rational argument can demand anything of a man other than that he be true to himself. Moral disagreements are irresoluble, and we have to live with them.

There are certain kinds of decisions which this description fits very well. 'There's no accounting for tastes', and most of us can think of decisions which we have made, for which there is, quite literally, no accounting — not because they were irrational, but because they transcended rational considerations. An example might be the decision to follow this or that career — a 'vocation', we call it, meaning that God has summoned us personally to it — or the decision to marry the partner we did. On these decisions we could receive advice of a kind, but not *moral counsel*, for nobody else could put himself in our shoes and tell us whether we loved Elvira enough to marry her, or whether we enjoyed study enough to become a professional academic. But then these decisions were not 'moral' decisions in the normal sense. John cannot form a good opinion about whether Philip should marry Ann, but he can form an opinion about whether Philip should marry a divorcee. Moral judgements, unlike personal choices, belong to the public domain of reason. We evaluate other people's moral stances and we expect them to evaluate ours. We argue about them, even get angry about them, all of which presupposes some public criterion of right and wrong. This second account of moral disagreement is as inadequate as the first.

The Natural Ethic

There is a third traditional account which claims our attention. It was the accepted view of mediaeval Christianity, which got it from Platonic and Aristotelian philosophy, and in consequence it has had little favour in Protestant cultures. But recently there has been a revived interest in it. It is sometimes called 'natural teleology'; but I shall refer to it simply as 'the natural ethic'.

It is possible to agree entirely on the facts of the case, and yet disagree about how it should be described. 'The government acted to protect the dairy industry', we imagine someone saying, 'by disposing of surplus dairy produce.' While another person may say: 'So much food was wasted!' The descriptions differ, because they make use of different categories. But that is because they presuppose different views of what the world actually contains. Two men look on milk: one sees it as 'produce', a sort of artefact of the dairy 'industry'; the other sees it as 'food'. But the one, in seeing it as food, cannot prevent himself thinking that it has a purpose: food is *for* nourishment. And that in turn commits him to seeing it as a 'waste' when it is thrown into the sea. The other, seeing it as produce, is equally bound to infer that milk has no natural purpose, since the purpose of produce is simply the purpose that its producer has had for it. Indeed, in describing milk as 'produce', he declares that 'food' does not really exist, not at any rate as a *natural* kind of thing. In his context of thought 'food' could only describe a use to which human agents might decide to put this or that product or this or that raw material. To call upon a traditional Greek distinction: one sees food as a category that exists 'in nature', the other as a category that exists only 'in convention'.

The natural ethic offers us this account of moral disagreement: that when men look on the world as a whole they see different things. On the bare facts they may agree; but the structure of reality behind the facts they see quite differently, and this affects the way they describe and understand the facts. Is there such a thing as 'food', or only market produce? Is there rule and obedience, or only a social contract? Is there free gift, or only subtler forms of exchange? Are there natural ties, or only voluntary associations? At this metaphysical level many of the most profound and painful moral disagreements arise.

It is my purpose in this essay to make a case for the natural ethic, mindful of the fact that I am in the presence of both science and theology, both of which have, for their own reasons, wished to deny it.

Voluntarism and Nominalism

Philosophers of science often stress that the Western scientific enterprise was born, at the end of the Middle Ages, in an intellectual milieu marked by two parallel movements in philosophy, 'voluntarism' and 'nominalism'.

'Voluntarism' was the belief that good and evil are determined, not by God's intellect but by his will. A sharp distinction was made between fact and value. Nature, as the expression of God's mind, was value-free; questions of good and evil turned on what it was God's will from time to time to command. If you are a voluntarist you can no longer say that God has made soya beans for our nourishment; you can only say that God made soya beans on the one hand, and now he commands that soya beans should feed us on the other, rather as he commanded the ravens to feed Elijah. Another way of expressing it would be that God's purposes are to be known only in his providential work in directing history, not in his creational work which precedes history.

From the philosophy of voluntarism science is held to have learned its detached approach to nature, as something to be 'put to the question', observed and understood, without love or obedience. Values may be imposed upon the natural order by technology, but not discerned within it. For the purposes of scientific thought natural teleology is rejected.

'Nominalism' on the other hand was the contention that 'kinds' of things do not have any real existence in nature, but are simply interpretations that the mind imposes on particular phenomena. The particular is real, the universal is a construct of the mind. God made me and you and the table, but it is man's mind, and not God's making, that classes the two of us as human and the table as inanimate. This philosophy made possible the pursuit of economy of explanation. If kinds are conventional, and not natural, it is up to us how many of them we choose to retain in our understanding of the world. We may force as wide a range of phenomena into as limited a repertoire of categories as we feel we can get away with.

From this follows what has sometimes been called the 'fragmentation' of reality under the discipline of scientific investigation. A science limits the area of its interest to the range of phenomena which appear to be susceptible to its patterns of thinking. Two different sciences may cover the same ground, and each give what seems to be a complete description of it, and yet the descriptions do not coincide. Philosophies of science have often accounted for this by some theory of 'aspects' of reality: some of us may be familiar with the elaborate system propounded by Herman Dooyeweerd under the heading of 'sphere sovereignty'. But this is to reflect back onto nature what is really a fragmentation in knowledge. The Western world has chosen to know the universe in parts rather than as a whole, and in economy rather than in diversity; and this deliberate policy, while it has yielded an extraordinary degree of technical mastery, has bred its own kinds of confusion. Ethical confusion is endemic to this mode of knowledge, for if there is no agreed way of describing what we see, there can be no agreed way of responding to it.

Science and the Natural Ethic

This, then, is why it is often said that the natural ethic received its death-wound at the end of the Middle Ages from that infant Hercules, the scientific revolution, then lying in its cradle. The first principle of the natural ethic is that reality is given to us, not simply in discrete, isolated phenomena, but in kinds. Things have *a natural meaning*. It is not a matter of interpretation to say that the table is an inanimate artefact while you and I are human beings; it is a matter of correctly discerning what is the case. The second principle is that these given kinds themselves are not isolated from each other, but relate to each other in a given pattern within the order of things. To know what *that* thing is is to know what *kind* of thing it is, and to know what *kind* of thing it is is to know how it fits into the whole, that is to say, what it is *for*. Things have *a natural purpose*. In understanding the natural purpose of a thing, we attend to its claims on us, and so are able to deliberate on our response to that claim. But with both these principles the philosophical revolution of the late Middle Ages tried to dispense.

It tried, but did it succeed? Science today, fully integrated into a world-view which accepts as an almost unquestionable premise the theory of evolution, can be seen to have done no more than substitute one species of teleology for another. Those who regard the nominalist-voluntarist revolution as a magnificent liberation of thought for 'masterful objectivity' may feel that the dog has returned to its vomit.[1] But we may

---

1. See Reflection B: The Views of T. F. Torrance

wonder whether the dog ever left its vomit. Some kinds of scientific description simply cannot be done non-teleologically. Biological and zoological descriptions are classic examples. How would you describe the digestive organs without saying that they were *for* digestion, or the tail of a horse without saying that it was *for* protection from flies? It was these sciences that espoused evolutionary thinking earliest and most determinedly, for they needed some teleological principle to make sense of their own work.

And then, too, while attempting to make all kinds relative, did scientific thought not absolutize to an extraordinary degree the categories of observer and observed? One form of this absolutism was 'humanism', which set mankind, the observer, over against all nature, the observed. But as the scope of science has extended to include humanity itself, humanism has been superseded by the same absolutism in new and more alarming forms. The observing and manipulating mind itself becomes something set absolutely over against the world. So far from abolishing metaphysics, the scientific approach to reality has only exchanged one set of metaphysical suppositions for other and more questionable ones.

But if the philosophical programme that gave birth to science was incapable of consistent fulfilment, we are relieved of a nagging anxiety. If scientific knowledge were a way of knowing the world that could be carried through consistently, we would have to choose between this kind of deliberately fragmented knowledge and the perception of the world as an integrated whole that our faith demands of us. The intellectual dividedness which all of us who have learned to know in both ways have experienced, would then be a wound beyond healing. But if it turns out that scientific objectivism is bound to serve *some other way* of knowing the world, then there is a possibility that it can be made to serve the Christian way. Once we see that the description of things with fluid categories and without teleology will never be a final description, then we can allow the usefulness of such description as a kind of thought-experiment to achieve a greater clarity of knowledge-in-detail. If we decide, as men of faith, that milk is not simply dairy-produce but food, then we can consider it also, though in a hypothetical and provisional way, as dairy produce. Provided we know that this is an experimental distortion of thought, not the essence of the thing, we can gain knowledge by looking through the distorting lens. It remains to us then to reintegrate what we see through the lens into the total pattern of understanding; and that, I suppose, is why it is thought proper for us, as representatives of so many disciplines, to discuss the questions of ethics, not in our separate disciplines, but together.

History — Revelation and Eschatology

Thinkers who understand the development of Western thought in this way, whether they welcome it or deplore it, are inclined to ascribe a good deal of the credit for it to Christianity.

It is true that for more than a millennium of Christian life and thought the late-Platonic unity of fact and value remained unchallenged in the Western church (as it still does in the Eastern); but that, it is said, only shows how slow Christianity was to emancipate itself from Hellenic tutelage and enter into its Jewish heritage. The sundering of fact and value was already implicit in the Old Testament conception which we call 'salvation history', the idea that meaning and worth were not to be found in the stabilities of nature but in the dynamisms of history. This conception reappears in Christianity in two forms. On the one hand it underlies the notion of a *historical revelation* of the meaning of the universe in the incarnation of the Son of God. On the other hand it underlies the belief that all history is to reach its goal at the *final intervention* of God and the establishment of his kingdom.

The voluntarist-nominalist movement of the fourteenth century has more to its credit than the fostering of scientific thought. It was the philosophical inspiration also for the Reformers. It gave them the tools to attack the Thomist epistemology which allowed that in principle (and in fairness to St. Thomas one should stress the phrase 'in principle'), natural man might perceive natural values and natural meanings without the aid of revelation. To this the Reformers reacted with a powerful and authentically Christian stress on the decisiveness of revelation. But revelation for them was really a Christological matter: to question the need of revelation was to question the need of Christ. The meaning of the world, the 'Logos', came down at Christmas; the man without Christmas is a man without meaning. The bestowal of meaning is part of God's saving work in history, for in nature man can discern no meaning.

What the Christian doctrine of revelation does for natural

meaning, its eschatological expectation does for natural purpose. Within Christianity one cannot think or speak about the meaning of the world without speaking also of its destined transformation. The problem of evil is met, not by asserting a profound cosmological order in the present, but by confident announcement of God's purposes for the future. He who has come to earth as the meaning, has come also as the Purpose or Fulfilment. To understand the first coming of Christ it is necessary to expect the second coming.

There are, of course, notoriously, two ways of living in expectation. We can believe in the value of intermediate transformation, 'preparing the way of the Lord', and so commit ourselves to a life of activity; or we can feel that the ultimate transformation renders all penultimate change irrelevant, and so resign ourselves to a life of hopeful suffering. But what these two attitudes have in common is far more important than what differentiates them. They both take a negative view of the *status quo*. There is no natural purpose to which we can respond in love and obedience. The destiny of nature has to be imposed on it, either by our activity or by God's. The purpose of the world is outside it, in that new Jerusalem which is to descend from heaven prepared as a bride for the bridegroom.

This description of the Christian impact on the natural ethic would meet with fairly wide acceptance, among those who deplore it as well as among those who welcome it. Yet I am bound to think that there is much of importance that it leaves out.

To take the point about revelation first. Revelation in history is certainly the lynchpin of Christian epistemology. But epistemology is not the same thing as ontology, however often the Protestant world may have confused the two. 'Nature' may be contrasted with 'revelation' as an epistemological programme; or it may be contrasted with 'history' to make an ontological distinction.[2] The important epistemological points that the Reformation had to make must not be allowed to shelter a destructive and semi-Christian ontology. It is one thing to say that until the Word became incarnate, man could discern no meaning in nature; quite another to say that until the Word became incarnate nature had no meaning. Revelation is the solution to man's blindness, not to nature's emptiness. True, man's blindness is itself part of a disruption within nature, which we call the fall. But the very

2. See Reflection A: 'The Natural' in Theology

fact that nature can be called disrupted and disordered shows that it cannot be inherently meaningless. In its earliest days the church was puzzled to find some within its midst believing that the world was made by an evil divinity, hostile to the God of redemption. In rejecting this speculation it made a sharp and necessary distinction between the idea that the world was simply chaotic and, what it understood the gospel to teach, that the world was an ordered creation tragically spoiled. Protestantism, in making the epistemological issue supreme over the ontological, has often tended to upset the balance that the Fathers struck.

Christian eschatology, too, to take up the second point, has to be seen in the light of the doctrine of creation. Christianity is an eschatological faith, having as its central theme the experience and hope of redemption from evil. But this redemption is not to be understood dualistically as the triumph of a good redeemer-god over an evil creator-god. It is because God is the creator of nature that he does, and will, redeem nature from its state of corruption. He who is the Saviour of the world is also the 'Logos', 'through whom all things were made'. He is the Second Adam, restoring that which the First Adam lost. Creation and redemption are not in hostile antithesis, but in complementarity, each providing the context in which we understand the other.

Balance between Nature and History

When thought fails to keep the Christian balance between meaning given in the natural order and meaning revealed in the course of history, it is at the mercy either of a static naturalism or an indeterminate belief in progress.

There are 'natural ethics' with which Christianity can have nothing to do. The respect for given orders can easily become a form of idolatry. The family, the state, the animal world, the mountains, the stars in heaven, man himself, can all command our love and allegiance in a way that allows no understanding of their proper place in the scheme of things. We love what is, only because we mistake it for something that it is not. We suppose that our tribe is the whole or the chief of mankind, we suppose that the planets fashion our destinies, we suppose that man is the master of all things. Much has been honoured as 'natural' that is purely conventional, the product of certain passing historical circumstances, and in this way great oppression has been laid on the souls of men. But not even a natural ethic that was entirely obedient to the revealed doctrine of creation could suffice as a complete moral guide in itself. The natural order makes claims upon us, which we must recognise and attend to; but the claims are generic, and in some situations we confront more than one of them. It may seem to us that seals have to be conserved; but so does the family and community life of Newfoundland seal-hunters. Man, too, is a creature with his own natural meaning and purpose, and part of that purpose is to exercise authority over the rest of nature. While we must certainly insist that his authority cannot be properly exercised unless he has a real understanding and love for nature, nevertheless he does have real discretion and a capacity to make choices which are not given inherently in the structure of nature itself.

And to these considerations we must add one more: in our actual situation in salvation history, we are dealing as fallen men with a fallen nature. Both we and nature come under the judgement of the God who created us, and that judgement is reflected in an ascetic series of duties and vocations which stand in a paradoxical relation to natural goals and functions. Thus we are required to 'hate' our father and our mother, our wife, children, brothers and sisters, and even our own life, in order to be Christ's disciples. Allowing for the element of rhetoric in this, we must still recognize a demand which falls quite outside the scope of the natural order, and, because the natural order itself is in rebellion against God, runs counter to it. Again, there is the possibility of a calling to singleness, 'making ourselves eunuchs', as Jesus puts it, for the kingdom of heaven's sake; and here too we have to recognise an eschatological demand which runs counter to the course which nature indicates.

We cannot allow ourselves, then, to champion an ethic in which everything is given in nature, nothing is to be revealed in history. But then neither can we take the other route, abandoning altogether the given values in favour of a solely eschatological outlook.

The Reformers avoided the consequences of their formal abandonment of natural value because they held so strongly to the decisive revelation of God in past history, which, including as it did the Scriptures as well as the Christ himself, in effect allowed them to have their cake and eat it. They still recognized given natural values, though not under that description, because they recognised Christ.[3] But when belief in a determinative past revelation was abandoned, the real implications of forsaking nature began to be apparent. The result was an open-ended belief in progress.

Belief in progress can be thought of as 'salvation history' without salvation. There is a general optimism, but no understanding of history as the restoring of what was lost, the recovery of things as they were always supposed to be. Value and meaning now arise from the very fact of transformation itself; there is no other criterion, other than the simple fact of change, by which we can judge good and evil. '"Progressive' and 'reactionary' become the standard terms of praise and blame. Despite its optimism, it is to the doctrine of progress that we must ascribe a large part of the anxiety and comfortlessness of our times. For when the future is known only as the negation of what is, and not as the more profound affirmation of its true structure, then it is simply alien to us. We cannot view it with hope, for hope requires some point of identification between the thing hoped for and the one who hopes for it. The only ways of facing the future are with fear or with the wild, self-destructive excitement which can grip a man when he stands on the edge of an unplumbed abyss.

Between Naturalism and Historicism — Race

One could choose many examples of how Christian ethics finds its way between a static naturalism and an unbridled historicism. I choose a familiar, perhaps a hackneyed one, in which the actual moral judgement involved is likely to be uncontroversial among us, but in which the Christian church has been both brave and effective. I speak, of course, of racism. There are two kinds of racial prejudice that have earned that name. On the one hand there is what is sometimes also called 'tribalism'. It is a naive naturalist philosophy, in which the race or the tribe is felt to have more importance in the structure of things than mankind as a whole, probably because it is more limited and so more easily conceivable. The race is known and loved as a natural kind. Life is lived in obedience to the fragmented good which this kind reveals. It is a simple man's vice, one manifestation of the xenophobia

---

3. The fact that some Reformation thinkers (notably Calvin, and later Hooker) had a place for the traditional doctrine of Natural Law, does not invalidate this generalisation about the tendencies of Protestantism.

which has always characterized the sheltered and the inexperienced. On the other hand there is the racism which motivated the Nazis, and today motivates at least one Western society, springing from a historicist philosophy. This is a vice of the sophisticated. It recognizes the fact that mankind is greater than the tribe, but it accords the kind, as it is given in nature, no love or allegiance. The existence of the human kind can have no point except in the light of a proposal to turn it into something else. But as all of what is traditionally called mankind cannot be included in the transformation of man into superman, the boundaries of humanity have to be kept fluid. The scheme of things can be reorganized in the service of a developing economic or scientific civilization to which only some of mankind can be admitted.

The Christian response to racism has appealed both to nature and to historical freedom. Christians have pointed to Christ, the Son of Man and God become man, to establish the worth of every man. On the one hand we cannot continue to elevate the tribe above the human race when we see how the Saviour of the world broke through the most intransigent tribalism to extend the offer of salvation to the ends of the earth. Our reading of the natural phenomena has to be controlled by what happened, by the Syrophoenician woman and by the vision of St. Peter. On the other hand we cannot treat the significance of humanity as a mere historical relativity when we believe that God has made humanity his own. Here is a category now that can never be transcended in history; but as soon as we have said that, we have asserted something about the structure of reality, not simply as it is becoming, but as it is given.

Tensions in Evangelical Ethics

This has some bearing on a disagreement which has disturbed our own small circles in recent years, between those who urge upon us a 'kingdom' ethic and those who support a 'creation' ethic. Neither kingdom nor creation can be known independently of each other. He who is called the King of kings is also called the Second Adam: nature and history in him are not divided. We would be foolish to allow ourselves to be polarised in this way, and even more foolish to conceive of such a polarisation in terms of Left and Right, as though the very profound philosophical issue involved could be summed up in a political cliché.

However, we may suggest in conclusion that there may be a legitimate division of interest among us that might appear to line us up in naturalist and historicist camps. We have to proclaim the gospel in different cultural and philosophical contexts. Many of us have deep sympathy with the problems of the Third World, tyrannical regimes, oppressive family and tribal structures, maldistribution of resources, and so on, and, speaking authentically to the static naturalisms which have produced and aggravated such problems, will talk eschatologically of transformation, and even, with a daring but possible expropriation of language, of 'revolution'. Others of us are concerned chiefly with the problems of the Western world, the abuses of technology, the threat to the family, the dominance of financial power, and so on, and find themselves needing constantly to point to the *data* of created nature. No doubt there is a temptation here: it is easy for the one group to think of the other as 'conservative' or 'radical'. But whenever we do this we exclude one side of the nature-history balance, and condemn our own stance to being less Christian for lack of that balance. I hope that in this conference we can make the mental and spiritual effort required of us to think beyond the issues that are all-important to ourselves at the moment and to learn to appreciate each other's proper concerns. As we do so we will approach nearer the point where we can grasp the Christian metaphysic in its wholeness and realize its significance for ethics.

Reflections

Conferences, especially if they are good ones, have a way of catching one's thought at a moment of transition. This poses a problem for 'the book of the conference': either the author rewrites his contribution entirely in the light of six months' more wrestling with his problems, or else he lets it stand as a kind of action snapshot, resigning himself to its unposed, provisional character. The subjects touched on in this lecture will continue to perplex me for some time yet, so I have been reasonably content to take the latter way, merely excising irrelevancies and one outright error. But discussions at the conference convinced me that, if I was to make myself understood, I must offer some clarification and defence at one or

two points, and I have tried to meet that need in these reflections. I owe a word of thanks to those who pressed me hard in
argument, forcing me to think further, but especially to my
wife, Joan, who opened my eyes to these problems in the first
place.

A   'The Natural' in Theology

The term 'natural' has two proper uses in Christian theology:
one ontological, opposed to 'historical' ('history' being used
in the Hegelian sense of *purposive* history), the other
epistemological, opposed to 'revealed'. (There is also a third,
improper use, in which 'natural' stands for 'fallen'; on this,
more below.) What the two uses of 'natural' have in
common is that they refer to everything that is not the self-
giving of God in Jesus Christ. Natural knowledge is that
which does not depend directly on Jesus and on his appointed
witnesses, the apostles and prophets. The natural order is that
which is not brought about as the result of saving history. But
although 'the natural' is not a part of salvation through
Christ, neither is it opposed to it, for it is the work of the
same God, the creator and sustainer of all. In either case the
natural is presupposed by, and redeemed through, the work
of salvation: natural knowledge is restored by revelation, the
natural order of things by saving history.

The 'natural ethic' which was defended in this lecture is
'natural' in the ontological sense — that is, it derives from the
created order. With the natural *knowledge* of ethics the lecture was not concerned. Perhaps some would think it less
confusing, since the two uses are so important to distinguish,
to retain the term 'natural' only for epistemological purposes,
and to find some other — 'created' suggests itself — to do duty
in ontological contexts. Against this proposal, however, there
are three considerations which I have found decisive.

First, 'nature' and 'history' are common philosophical
terms, and their use enables us to speak more effectively to
important debates going on outside the church.

Secondly, we need a term broader than 'creation', one
which will include also what has commonly been designated
in Christian theology as 'providence' — that is, God's work
in history which is not directly purposive- or saving-history,
the work of preserving and sustaining the created universe.
Christian ethics finds it important to speak of a natural order

which embraces God's providential dispositions for fallen man (in the political realm, for example), and which is not confined to the primary forms in which man receives his created being. Failure to speak in this way leads to the quite untheological assumption, not without its advocates among those present at the conference, that these secondary forms of natural existence are simply the product of man's own constructive ingenuity.

Thirdly, the term 'natural' is used famously in the Authorised Version at 1 Cor. 2:14ff. to translate St. Paul's *psuchikos*: 'the natural man receiveth not the things of the Spirit of God'. At the High Leigh conference I was so unwise as to criticize this translation. Misled by the RSV and other modern versions as to the apostle's meaning, I took the Stuart translators to be guilty of a typically Protestant confusion of the natural with the fallen. But Paul was not speaking of fallen man in these verses, as his own interpretation of the *psuché-pneuma* contrast at 1 Cor. 15:44f. makes quite clear.

B   The Views of T. F. Torrance

I quoted the phrase 'masterful objectivity' from Professor Torrance's article, cited below. In the course of the conference Dr. David Cook persuaded me to look more carefully at Torrance's views and especially at his book *Theological Science*. It has been an exciting discovery.

The 'masterful objectivity' for which Torrance praises a somewhat idealised scientific enquiry is not a dispassionate attitude, but a selfless absorption in the object of enquiry based on the knowledge that God has made it. Nor does it force an arbitrarily conceived structure of kinds upon nature, but is wholly reponsive to the kinds which nature has in itself and will reveal to the enquirer. Thus the meaning of things is immanent to them, and naturally known. Not so their purpose. Value is conferred upon the creation by divine grace alone, and cannot be discerned immanently within it. The theory of natural teleology, purporting to trace the purposive interconnections of kinds, is rejected as a form of idolatry. Thus, measured by the late-mediaeval grid, Torrance counts as a voluntarist, but not a nominalist.

Torrance's objection to natural teleology is that it fails to distinguish the creation from the creator, an objection which is valid against some, but certainly not against all versions of

the theory. In return we must object that the value supposed-
ly conferred upon nature by divine grace is a mere abstraction
unless it can be recognised, with or without the help of revelation, in the purposive interconnections of kinds. Only so can
we see that the universe is an 'order', and affirm, with the
creator, that it is 'very good'. Without the possibility of this
discernment, the doctrine of creation is destined to drop out
of sight, and man's autonomous will-to-mastery must take
over, imposing human purposes where God apparently omitted to impose divine ones. Which, of course, is the story of
Western culture since the Reformation.

When revelation is barred in principle from com-
municating any substantial information about the kinds in
nature, and when science is barred in principle from observing purposive interconnections among the kinds, the possibility of a unified knowledge of the natural order is lost. We are
left to the fragmented vision afforded by a plurality of
arbitrarily-defined sciences. The objection we raised against
Dooyeweerd applies even more forcibly to Torrance: God's
creation should not be held responsible for a fragmentation
which is really due to the problem of *knowledge* in fallen
mankind. (On this, Rahner's article, cited below, is important.) Theology is committed to pursuing a unified vision. The
devastating implications of scientific fragmentation for
Christian ethics are not observed by Torrance, probably
because he measures all science by the norm of physics and
does not concern himself with the human sciences, where the
issue arises most sharply.

Reading List

Owen Barfield, *Saving the Appearances: A Study in
    Idolatry* (New York, 1965).
Herman Dooyeweerd, *The Christian Idea of the State*
    (1936) (Nutley, N. J., 1968).
George Grant, 'In Defence of North America', in
    Technology and Empire: Perspectives on North America
    (Toronto,1969).
Karl Rahner, 'Theology as Engaged in an Interdisciplinary
    Dialogue with the Sciences', in *Theological Investigations
    XIII* (London, 1975).
T. F. Torrance, 'The Influence of Reformed Theology on the

Development of Scientific Method', in *Theology in Reconstruction* (London, 1965).
— *Theological Science* (Oxford, 1969).

Questions for Discussion

1   Are there matters of fact which carry with them a moral demand? (For example: If Jones promised to Smith . . .)

2   Is scientific description bound to over-simplify the truth?

3   Is what we see through Christ in nature different from what we would see otherwise?

4   If we cannot *balance* creation ethics and kingdom ethics, what *can* we do with them?

Chapter Two
Using the Bible in Ethics
I. Howard Marshall

CHAPTER TWO
Using the Bible in Ethics

Basic Assumptions

I START WITH THE ASSUMPTIONS (A) THAT *SCRIPTURE HAS something relevant to say on the subject of ethics,* and (b) that *as evangelical Christians we are bound by the authority of Scripture.* Both these propositions need a little amplification.

(a) The Bible is certainly very much concerned with ethics, that is to say, with the ways in which goodness and righteousness should be shown by individuals and groups in their inter-relations. Indeed, so great is the stress in the Bible on ethics that it has been possible in the past for Christianity to be regarded as not much more than a code of morality with a certain dash of piety tossed in to give it a faintly religious aroma, and in the present for the admitted vertical dimension to be transmuted into horizontal terms: to love God is nothing but loving your neighbour. That both of these viewpoints are ill-conceived does not alter the fact that there is sufficient morality in the Bible to give them a semblance of credibility.

(b) As for the authority of Scripture, this is more questionable in the Christian world at large, although it is accepted without much argument by Evangelicals. I will simply comment that even among non-evangelicals there remains a lingering suspicion that the Bible is authoritative; sermons are

still based on biblical texts, and if a preacher or scholar dis-
agrees with what Scripture says, he usually feels compelled to
produce some good reasons for his disagreement. On the
other hand, Evangelicals sometimes do merely lip service to
the authority of Scripture, and they have their own way of
wriggling out from under it when they find it disagreeable.

Problems in Using the Bible Today

What then are our problems in using the Bible in ethics?
    1. The first of them is that *the ethical problems which con-*
front us today may not be directly presented in the Bible. This
may happen in several ways, of which I offer one or two
examples.
    First, there is the development of *new scientific techniques*
which were not envisaged in biblical times. These arise particularly in the area of birth — the use of contraceptives, the
practice of artificial insemination by husband or another
donor, the possibilities of so-called test-tube babies, the problem of abortion, the potential of genetical engineering, and
the like. We cannot simply read off answers to such problems
from the Bible.
    Second, there is the development of *new structures in*
society which were not envisaged in biblical times or appear
only marginally. The Bible does contain some teaching on the
Christian and the state, but that state is usually a monarchy
or empire or oligarchy; sometimes the monarchy is presented
as a theocracy. The question of the obedience of the individual to a state which is a democracy is scarcely raised, nor
is the general question of whether one type of state is
preferable to another. The problem of the participation of the
individual in the processes of government scarcely arises.
Other structures are not mentioned. We hear something about
master-slave relationships and commercial relationships, but
the existence of trade unions does not arise (the silversmiths'
guild at Ephesus (Acts 19:24f.) was more probably an
employers' federation), and we hear nothing of multi-national
companies and the problems of loyalties that they raise. 'You
cannot serve two masters', said Jesus, but many people cannot avoid the competing claims of different masters.
    Third, there is the recognition of the so-called right of
groups to achieve their aims by *methods that involve conflict*
and the use of violence in the broadest sense. Trade unions

employ industrial action in order to achieve their aims by compelling employers or the government or the public at large to give them what they want. On a wider level armed revolution takes place in some countries in order to achieve a change of ruler; this was not of course unknown in the ancient world, but is it reckoned with in New Testament ethics? Fourth, there is the problem of *the Christian living in a state which follows standards different from his own.* If he is involved in the life of that society, how does he reconcile the performance of his Christian duty with his public duty? For example, a social worker may privately believe in the sinfulness of divorce, but may be expected to recommend it as a possible solution in cases of marital conflict. A person who believes in forgiveness of one's enemies may find himself acting as a judge and unable to forgive the convicted criminals who appear before him, or as a soldier under compulsion to kill or maim the enemies of his country.

2. The points I have discussed so far are for the most part examples of problems that arise because we live in a different world from the biblical world, and hence have to reckon with situations that are not the object of ethical discussion in the Bible. Another set of problems arises from *the character of the biblical revelation.*

First, even in terms of its own time *the Bible is not an ethical textbook*, attempting to cover systematically the legal, social and ethical problems of its time. Obvious evidence of this point is the way in which the Jewish teachers found it necessary to clarify and up-date the pentateuchal legislation so that it would work in their own situation. The New Testament teaching is also incomplete, and its detailed discussions are confined to a handful of topics, presumably the ones found most pressing in the early days of the church.

Second, the biblical teaching is given very much *in terms of divine revelation,* with a certain amount of application of principles found elsewhere in Scripture to provide for new situations, a certain amount of appeal to 'nature' or natural law, and a certain amount of appeal to commonsense, custom and the like. All this raises the question of *the justification of a Christian ethic.* Suppose that a Christian wishes to take a stand on adultery in a secular society. What the Bible gives him is a categorical, divine condemnation. Does he justify the wickedness of adultery in a secular situation by appealing to the divine fiat? Or does he attempt to show, in a manner which may go beyond biblical teaching but has some basis in it, that adultery produces undesirable effects in society and thus in effect try to show why God legislated against it? In short, how far can an appeal to a divinely revealed ethic cut any ice in a society which disputes the authority of God or the Bible? Can the biblical basis of morality be authoritative for people who do not accept the authority of the Bible?

Third, there is the hermeneutical question of *whether biblical ethics are intended to apply to mankind in general*, to a state which acknowledges the authority of God and/or the Bible, or merely to the godly individual. Consider again the case of divorce: is our problem simply that Jesus' prohibition of divorce applies to his followers, and that a different standard is countenanced for society at large? In fact, different sections of biblical teaching may be meant for different constituencies, and we have the problem of whether it is all meant to be universally applicable in the modern world.

Fourth, there is the question of *the permanence of the various aspects of biblical ethics*. This problem arises especially in relation to the Old Testament law parts of which are explicitly said to be no longer applicable in the New Testament era, such as the sacrificial legislation, the rules for hygiene and tithing. The New Testament writers regarded some parts of the Old Testament as still binding upon Christians, as Rom. 13:8-10, for example, makes clear. But how does one differentiate? The old distinction between moral, ceremonial and civil laws is a loose one, and I can see no evidence that it is a biblical distinction. But the same problem also arises in respect of the New Testament teaching on ethics: how much of this is intended to be of permanent and universal applicability, and how much is meant for specific people in particular circumstances?

3. A further set of problems may be broadly called *hermeneutical*. These arise at various levels.

First, there is the *exegetical* problem of determining precisely what a given biblical text *meant* for the original readers. There can be difficulties of text and vocabulary, sentence construction and so on — all the problems that arise in an exegetical discussion. Along with this there may be the question of different understandings of the text at different times. We can distinguish in theory between the significance that a given text in the Old Testament may have had for the original hearers or readers and the significance which it had when read by Jesus or the early Christians who proceed to use the text in some way in their own teaching. I think that it would be true to say that the primary application which Paul makes of Deut. 25:4 in 1 Cor. 9:9 is a different one from that which Moses intended his hearers to make of it.

Thus even within the Bible itself we find the beginnings of my second problem which is that of *determining the significance* or application of the text to our own situation. You will note that I am being careful with my terms here. Contrary to the view of some interpreters I am assuming, along with E. Hirsch, *Validity in Interpretation* (New Haven, Yale University Press, 1967), that we can distinguish between the meaning and the significance of a text, the former of which is fixed and, in theory at least, objectively determinable, while the latter may vary according to the situation and character of the receptor of the text. A text has one meaning, but may have varying significance. (This way of putting it is no doubt a simplification, and a certain amount of clarification and qualification may be called for, but I feel fairly confident that the principle is basically a right one.)

Third, for most simple folk, among whom I should number myself, the significance of a text flows out of its meaning. That is why, for example, biblical interpreters in general repudiate the allegorical interpretation of non-allegorical texts, since the allegorical interpretation assigns to the text a significance which bears little or no relation to its original meaning and significance. But problems arise when *the meaning of a text may be unacceptable to the modern interpreter.* This can happen in various ways. If we were to read in an ancient text 'Thou shalt commit adultery', we would respond in all probability by rejecting the suggestion as immoral. If we know that the statement is from a secular source, or that its author is a wicked person, we have no hesitation in rejecting the command. If we do not know anything about the source, we draw the conclusion that it must be a wicked person who wrote it, and in both cases we act in this way because the text conflicts with a moral standard that we have come to accept. We may, of course, adopt a more sophisticated approach. We may ask *why* the author made this statement. I shall let the cat's head out of the bag by reminding you that this statement does actually occur in an early printed book, and that its cause is nothing more than a printer's error. But it is also possible that a writer may make the statement to shock us, and to make us ask ourselves why we assume that adultery is wrong so that we may perhaps come to a better-grounded understanding of a principle that we have accepted without thinking very deeply about it; or perhaps again a writer may believe that in certain circumstances, or rather (to use the trendy word) in certain 'situations', adultery is right, and be trying to persuade us accordingly. We then consider his arguments, assuming that he does develop and defend his statement, and assess them by our own moral standards. And we feel free to accept or reject the statement, letting our own conscience be the ultimate arbiter. But now, having let the cat's head out of the bag, let me allow its body to follow by reminding you that my text 'Thou shalt commit adultery' is in fact found in an early edition of the Bible. True, it is nothing more than a printer's error, but what do we do with other statements of a similar kind when we find them as a genuine part of the Bible? I open the Old Testament almost at random and discover that during the conquest of Palestine Joshua fought against Libnah, 'and the Lord gave it also and its king into the hand of Israel; and he smote it with the edge of the sword, and every person in it; he left none remaining in it' (Jos. 9:30). Plainly Joshua and the author of this text thought that it was the Lord's will that the people of Libnah should be massacred (see Deut. 20:10-18), and that the Lord enabled Joshua to carry out the massacre. There is no problem if we read about something like this in an ancient historian; but it is a problem when we read something like it in the Bible and find that it goes against our moral sense. Here the meaning of the text seems to be morally unacceptable. (I am aware of the reason given for this kind of genocide in Deut. 20:18; but is it a principle on which modern Christians would feel able to justify the practice?)

Fourth, we have the problem that *the thinking of the Bible may not correspond with ours.* There is the case in 1 Cor. where Paul commands that a certain person who has committed incest is to be 'handed over to Satan' for the destruction of the flesh at a solemn church meeting. Later in the same epistle he comments on the possibility of members of the church having fellowship with demons by participating in pagan cult meals, in the same way as they can have fellowship with the Lord in the Lord's Supper, and he intimates that God may act in judgement against those who thus provoke him to jealousy. Indeed he says that disrespect for the Lord's Supper has led to the illness and death of some of the members. Whether or not we accept this way of thinking in theory, the vast majority of us certainly do not accept it in practice. Excommunication may happen, but I have never heard of a modern church in this country actually handing over one of its members to Satan, and I do not think that any reputable evangelical pastor has ever suggested to a grief-stricken widow that the reason for her husband's sudden death was that he had provoked the Lord to jealousy or had partaken of the sacrament in an unworthy manner. I suggest to you that our practice speaks more loudly than our possible private beliefs in such matters as these. In practice we do not believe that this kind of thing happens, and we certainly do not behave as if we believed it. There is a different kind of thinking at certain points in the Bible.

Fifth, there is the problem that *the teaching in the Bible may vary in its different parts.* I have spoken of the legitimacy of the total ban placed on pagan populations in Joshua. But we have only to turn to Amos to find stirring denunciations of exactly the same kind of conduct committed by pagan nations, and there is not the slightest doubt that had contemporary Israel acted in the same way Amos would have been as fearless in condemning it as he was in inveighing against the injustice that existed in the commercial and social life of the people. There are differences of level and content in the ethical teaching of the Bible, and in the understanding of God's will that lies behind the ethical teaching.

All these points build up to a situation of considerable complexity, and it is time now to consider what may be done in the light of it.

Some Contemporary Approaches

I turn therefore to a listing of *some possible approaches* that arise in dealing with the problem of using the Bible in ethics.

1. *Extreme biblicism* takes the Bible literally and typifies the popular understanding of 'fundamentalism': all the Bible (with the exception of certain parts of the Old Testament) is true and prescriptive on the same level. This is the sort of approach which has led, to cite some of the more extreme cases, to the prescription that women must wear their heads covered at worship, or to an insistence on the capital punishment of murderers, or to a refusal to take the oath in a court of law.

Its shortcomings are manifest. First, it is *tacitly selective* in its approach to the Bible. It accepts certain prescriptions and not others. Second, it is often *guilty of inadequate exegesis,* since it tends to be wedded to an unscholarly approach to the text. Third, it can produce *ethical results which are out of harmony with modern ethical insights.* There is of course nothing wrong with that: a biblical ethic may sharply challenge modern ethical systems where these fall short of the divine will. But my point is rather that the biblicistic approach may lead to ethical prescriptions which are out of harmony with an approach based on the Christian church's development of the biblical teaching: for example, modern rejection of capital punishment may arise from a development of biblical teaching regarding the dignity of man, the possibility of divine forgiveness, and so on. Put otherwise, the biblicistic approach fails to appreciate the character of the Bible which is such that certain parts of the biblical teaching may render other parts obsolete for the present day: the generally recognised abolition of certain parts of the Old Testament law in the light of the New Testament revelation is but one aspect of a wider phenomenon.

2. The opposite extreme is typified by D. E. Nineham's book on *The Use and Abuse of the Bible.* Here what is emphasised is *the cultural gap between the thinking of the biblical world and the modern world,* and it is evident that for Nineham this gap is so great that the Bible can scarcely be used at all today. The whole of the book is a development of this theme. I do not want to go into the book in detail. It must suffice to raise the fundamental question whether the gap is as great as Nineham makes it out to be. His criterion appears to be that what is unacceptable to modern man is of no direct use today. But one might observe, first, that the thinking of Christians is in fact to a large extent already determined by the thinking of the Bible, so that it might be hard for them to distinguish between the biblical and other influences upon their total world-view. It seems possible to achieve a biblical world-view which will at the same time do justice to the insights of modern science. It is in fact the task of systematic theology to do precisely this, and it is somewhat sweeping to declare in effect that the venture is an impossible one from the outset. Second, one must insist that the biblical world-view may act as a challenge to the beliefs of so-called modern man. If modern man thinks of himself as judging the Bible in the light of his own beliefs or even of his own agnosticism, he may find that the Bible is calling his own outlook into question and pointing to dimensions of reality

of which he is unaware. One can point out, for example, how Christian thinking brought a needed challenge to the male-dominated society of first-century Judaism, and performs a similar service today, and that the fundamental challenges to Nazism and to racism generally have been based on a biblical outlook.

3. Another type of approach, which recognises the sort of problem raised by Nineham, and is indeed probably the source of his approach, is that of R. Bultmann and *the demythologising school.* This approach attempts to take what is expressed in the mythological language of the first century and translate it into another type of language which can speak meaningfully to modern man. The aim is a positive one, and perhaps we all practise it to some extent. Thus, if the biblical writers did in fact think of heaven as being 'up there' and of Jesus as literally ascending on a cloud that could take him all the way to heaven, we would most of us argue that this was an acted parable, and that in reality Jesus was moving to another dimension of reality. What I want to suggest is that we have perhaps reacted against a fundamentally valid insight in Bultmann's treatment because of three possibly extraneous factors. One is that Bultmann's approach was linked to *an extreme historical scepticism* not only about the miraculous elements in the biblical narrative but also about the presentation of Jesus and the early church in general. This scepticism is completely unjustified, and there is good reason to adopt a much more favourable attitude to the historicity of the documents. A second factor was Bultmann's *total rejection of the supernatural* which led to denial of the miracles, the resurrection, and the activity of the Holy Spirit. Here, however, is precisely one of the points where the biblical world-view may challenge the modern assumption of a closed universe, and we are not compelled to follow Bultmann here. The third factor is that Bultmann tied his thesis to *the idea of 'myth'*, affirming that biblical concepts were presented in the garb of timebound myths. His idea of what constituted myth was undoubtedly something of a ragbag, and here more careful definition is required. Whether he would have called Heidegger's philosophy a modern mythology I am not sure. Unfortunately, however, he used what is undoubtedly a pejorative term to refer to biblical ways of thinking.

I want to suggest that Bultmann might have done better to speak in terms of models or symbols of reality, and to make the point that what is expressed in terms of one kind of model

or symbol may also be expressed, and perhaps more meaningfully expressed, in terms of other models. There are times
when the older models may be the most appropriate ones for
communication. If a young child who cannot conceptualise
abstractly to any great extent asks me who God is or where
heaven is, I shall not communicate intelligibly with him by
stating that God is the ground of being or Being itself or that
heaven is not capable of being plotted on a space-time con-
tinuum. But if I tell him that God is like a father and that
heaven is 'up there', I shall convey some information to him
that is not totally misleading and which expresses for him, at
his level of comprehension, what can also be expressed in
more abstract terms for those who find the simple models
open to misunderstanding. In other words, the biblical expressions are valid in their own way, and so are the modern
expressions, although the latter need to be continually tested
and reformulated so that they are accurate translations of the
biblical expressions.

I believe, then, that this may be a helpful approach, and I
am suggesting that in fact we often practise it even though the
concept of demythologisation may be anathema to us. But it
is only fair to point out a difficulty. Whereas this approach
can take care of biblical concepts such as heaven and God
which lie outside our space-time frame of reference, *it is not
clear what we are to do with points where the Beyond im-
pinges upon our frame of reference.* Here I am thinking of
things like demon possession or the appearances of angels
where the biblical concepts take on historical form. Put
otherwise, it may not be too difficult to regard the angels in
heaven as pictorial representations of the glory of God, and
of his power and love streaming forth; it is more difficult to
transpose the actual appearance of an angel to Zechariah in
the temple or to Mary into the story of the development of an
inward conviction about the purpose of God. Any attempt to
use the transposing of models as a refinement of the Bult-
mannian programme which avoids its manifest shortcomings
must find a satisfactory answer to this difficulty.

4. In some of his writings J. L. Houlden stresses *the variety
of ethical positions* in the New Testament and the impossibility
of discovering any norm. Houlden illustrates this by looking
at two or three areas of New Testament ethical teaching and
shows the existence of development and variety. The sort of
conclusion that may be drawn from this type of approach is
that the Bible shows us examples of ethical thinking that may

be helpful but cannot be normative. We may see in general terms that ethics must be theologically based, but not much more than this.

5. A somewhat similar type of approach is to be found in J. T. Sanders who finds that *most of the New Testament ethical teaching is tied to outworn theological concepts* and cannot be made the basis for modern thinking: Jesus' ethics, for example, are based on the imminence of the kingdom of God, and stand or fall with the fulfilment of his expectation. Faced by such problems, writers of this outlook tend to investigate whether there is any general ethical principle which informs New Testament teaching as a whole and which appears to be in harmony with modern ethical consciousness. Sanders comes near to saying that the New Testament says nothing distinctive about ethics, and falls into the trap of thinking that what it says is therefore valueless. Other writers identify the principle of love for one's neighbour as the basic principle which comes to expression, sometimes imperfectly, in New Testament ethical teaching, and then claim that we are thrown back on this principle as our basic guide with which to approach modern problems.

The questioning of Houlden's and Sanders' position must take place at an exegetical level. I would query it at various points. First, we would want to ask *whether the different elements in New Testament teaching are so irreconcilable with one another.* May not the differences be due to the influence of different circumstances? Second, I would certainly want to differ from Sanders in *his understanding of the eschatological teaching of Jesus and the New Testament writers* which seems to be decidedly faulty. Third, I would assert that while the New Testament does take over statements common to secular ethical systems this in no way diminishes their value or their authority. Sanders is right to ask what is distinctive in the New Testament understanding; he is *wrong to imply that anything that is not distinctive is lacking in value.*

However, the positive value in this approach is that it alerts us to the need to account for the variety in biblical teaching and to see whether a fruitful synthesis is possible.

Towards an Evangelical Approach

Against this background we now turn to consider *the*

evangelical discussion of hermeneutics which has been con-
ducted by A. C. Thiselton, and which I have attempted to
develop in my own way in an article in *Third Way*. The
essence of this approach is to suggest that when we come to a
biblical exhortation *we must inquire into the underlying
theological and ethical principles* which are expressed in it,
and then proceed to work out how to translate those principles into appropriate exhortations for today.

If we adopt this approach we can easily see how much exhortation is the practical expression of concern and love for
one's neighbour.

A simple example would be the incident of footwashing in
Jn. 13 where Jesus tells his disciples that they ought to do to
one another what he has done to them (Jn. 13:14f.). There
are some Christian groups which follow his command literally, but the practice is not general. The changed conditions of
our culture mean that footwashing does not have the necessity, the significance, nor even the convenience which it had
in first-century Palestine. It is, however, abundantly plain
from the context that what Jesus was commanding his
disciples to do was to display humility and mutual love and
one appropriate way of doing this in the first century in
Palestine was by performing this service. So the principle in
the action is apparent, and we are to fulfil that principle by
showing humility and love in service for one another. We
may feel perhaps that we ought to find some modern
equivalent to the action which Jesus chose as a real example
of humble service and as a symbol of what we should be
always ready to do in other ways, but in fact we have not
done so, and perhaps if we did have such a symbolic action
we might fall into the temptation of thinking that in performing it we had fulfilled our Christian duty. For what it is
worth, however, I suggest that in a culture where the
automatic dishwasher is not yet the common status-symbol of
middle-class Christians, guests should relieve their hosts of
the task of washing up after partaking of a meal.

This is a comparatively simple example where we begin
from a biblical exhortation, analyse it to find the basic principle expressed, and then examine our culture to find appropriate ways of expressing the exhortation. In principle we
need to do this with all biblical ethical teaching.

Let me now make some comments on this method,
especially in relation to the problems and approaches outlined in the earlier part of the paper.

1. This approach to biblical ethical teaching *takes the authority of the Bible seriously.* Even where the text prescribes something that seems to be strange to us, we must still wrestle with the text to discover what it is really saying and then apply this to our own cultural situation. In this way the whole Bible will continue to speak its own word into our modern situation, and it will continually challenge the accepted life-style and easy assumptions of modern society. The biblical ethic will continue to find creative application.

2. This approach to biblical teaching *takes the variety in modern situations and cultures seriously.* What is appropriate in twentieth-century Britain may not be appropriate in other places and times, and our principle recognises that this is so; the significance of Scripture for each individual situation must be carefully worked out. There is nothing new about this concept; we implicitly recognise it when we admit that the same sermon may not meet the needs of different congregations.

3. This approach allows for the application of the biblical material to situations that are not specifically envisaged in the Bible, or to problems that do not receive sufficiently detailed attention. The task of the biblical moralist is *to extrapolate from Scripture to the particular ethical exhortations appropriate in different situations.* To be sure, there is a problem here. It may not be easy to start from the modern situation and discover what biblical teaching is relevent to it. The appropriate biblical principles may be locked up in material that at first sight has little or no resemblance to the modern problem. We must have a thorough general knowledge of the biblical material and the principles which it enshrines in order to have the teaching resources to apply to our contemporary problems.

4. In view of the differences between the biblical situations and problems and our own ones the common factors will be found in *principles that can be applied to both types of situation,* principles of sufficient generality to be applicable in a variety of circumstances. Often these principles may be clearly apparent and lie, as it were, on the surface of the text, so that we can do a fairly straight application to the modern situation; at other times, we may have to burrow more deeply in order to find them. Obviously many modern situations may have close biblical analogues; in such cases application is simple, although we must be careful not to draw hasty, superficial analogies. My concern is to draw attention to the areas

where at first Scripture seems to have nothing to say to us, and to claim that it does in fact have relevant teaching.

5. By this method we can overcome the cultural gap at one level. We are in effect carrying through a transformation of biblical teaching similar to that practised in the kind of 'evangelical alternative' to demythologising that I have described earlier. *We are no longer forced to take literally commands which are no longer applicable in changed circumstances.*

6. In the same way, we may have *an answer to the problem of the alleged lack of consistency in biblical teaching.* The existence of different law-codes and varying ethical commands may be simply the result of different application of the same basic principles in different situations. Two points arise:

(i) *Are the biblical ethical principles* underlying the surface application *consistent with one another?* Or do the differing applications reflect inconsistent principles?

(ii) Are the biblical principles reducible to, say, one basic principle, which would be that of love for one's neighbour? If so, do we need subsidiary principles, or can we dispense with them?

Paul certainly claims that the second part of the decalogue is reducible to the one commandment to love one's neighbour, and indeed he goes on to claim that if there is any other commandment it is summed up in this one (Rom. 13:8-10). *This does not, however, mean that the individual commandments can be dispensed with*; on the contrary it would seem that we need to be reminded what love means in concrete situations, and indeed what love itself means. For this we need guidance, and I would claim in broad terms that we need to be reminded about the character of man as a creature made in the image of God and as the sinner for whom Christ died, so that we may know how to love people as people. We also need the biblical doctrine of the community so that our love will not be purely individualistic but will take account of God's plan to create a people bound together by mutual love.

7. What I have said indicates that the Christian concept of love is *derived from the Christian revelation of God* and his will for his people. In other words, the command that we should love God is prior to the command that we should love our neighbour and gives content and meaning to it. We have,

therefore, a hierarchy of commandments, to love God, to love our neighbour, and to do so in specific ways. It can, therefore, be said that the principles which we shall expect to find underlying biblical ethics will arise out of the biblical revelation of God's love and in his commands to us to love him and one another. It is for guidance in the practical out-working of these commands that we turn to biblical ethics. Biblical ethics thus arise out of biblical theology. The nature and force of the commands arises out of the doctrine of God and the world which lies behind them. Their validity is therefore that of the biblical revelation itself, and a discussion of this point would lead us further afield than our present limited topic.

Nevertheless two further questions which arose from our preliminary discussion must be briefly answered.

8. *What is the status of biblical ethics in relation to secular-based ethics?* Humanists believe in the primacy of love and care for human beings as human beings. Can we not take our stance on that principle, and so seek common ground with secular moralists, and leave out the theology? Very often in practice we do this. We argue the case against euthanasia, for example, on general grounds rather than because we believe that God has forbidden us to take life in this way. But we should, I think, want to argue that the status and nature of persons is difficult, if not impossible, to uphold without the Christian basis, and that it is our duty to stress this in the long-term interests of ethics, even if we may ally with other defenders of what is right or argue against what is wrong on grounds that are less directly theological.

9. *Is progress in ethical thinking possible?* The familiar example is the way in which slavery is tolerated in the Bible, although the Bible contains the doctrines which were ultimately seen to render slavery unacceptable. In the same way, parts of the Bible may tolerate genocide, but the Bible as a whole contains the principles which render genocide unacceptable. The problem has two aspects. First, there is the presence in the Bible of divine commands to perform acts (such as genocide) which are unacceptable in the light of later biblical teaching on the love of God for all men. Second, there is the question whether specific commandments may not be regarded as examples of the law of love which are no longer appropriate and can be disregarded. In other words, might it not be possible for crucial biblical principles to be dismissed as being simply time-bound applications of the

biblical principle of love? It might be claimed, therefore, that my method is an example of 'thin-end-of-the-wedge-ism' and fraught with danger. However, I should want to argue against this rejoinder and protest that the existence of difficulties and risks is no argument against a method; an extreme biblicist approach runs the opposite danger of demanding absolute obedience to time-bound commandments, and this, one might say, is a case of 'thick-end-of-the-wedge-ism'. So far as the other point is concerned, that of attributing unloving commands to God, the problem is again wider than the question of ethics, and I submit that it is one for general theology.

I have not been able to tackle all the problems raised in my opening survey, but perhaps sufficient has been said by way of elucidation of a possible answer to the question of how we use the Bible in ethics. In effect I have concentrated on how to interpret the Bible; the problems that arise in applying it, thus interpreted, to contemporary ethical issues would require another paper or series of papers.

Reading List

J. L. Houlden, *Ethics and the New Testament* (Harmondsworth, 1973).

I. H. Marshall, 'Interpreting Scripture Today', *Third Way* 1:16 (1977).

D. E. Nineham, *The Use and Abuse of the Bible* (London, 1976).

O. O'Donovan, 'The Possibility of a Biblical Ethic', *TSF Bulletin* 67 (Autumn 1973), pp. 15-23.

id., 'Towards an Interpretation of Biblical Ethics', *Tyndale Bulletin* 27 (1976), pp. 54-78.

J. T. Sanders, *Ethics in the New Testament* (London, 1976).

A. Thiselton, 'Understanding God's World today', in J. R. W. Stott (ed.), *Obeying Christ in a Changing World: 1. The Lord Christ* (London, 1977), pp. 90-122.

Questions for Discussion

1   In what ways can we commend a biblical ethic in a society which does not accept the authority of the Bible?

2   Can any guidance for modern warfare be drawn from Deut. 20:10-18?

3   Is it true that 'certain parts of the biblical teaching may render other parts obsolete for the present day'?

4   How big is the cultural gap between the biblical world and the modern world? How would you counter the claim that it is so great that biblical teaching has largely lost its relevance for today?

5   Discuss the validity of the process of extracting ethical principles from biblical commands, as outlined in the closing part of the essay.

Chapter Three
From Christendom to Pluralism
John Briggs

From Christendom to Pluralism

Definitions

DOUBTLESS THE EMERGENCE OF PLURALISM HAS MUCH IN common with the more general process of secularization, the impact of permissiveness, the discounting of authority in favour of an all-sovereign relativism: indeed each and all of these are elements in our modern plurality of thought. But pluralism as such embraces further elements and requires, in consequence, more careful and precise definition. For the purpose of this paper, I take a pluralist state to be a state which, in its institutions, laws and culture, reflects the diversity of race, creed and heritage of its members, at least in some measure. In contradistinction, the unitary state is a state where common experience and belief allow the state itself to adopt a distinctive religious or philosophical stance in which it presumes to speak for all its members, and because of which, it feels able to require of them a uniformity of moral and religious practice. Whatever its degree of success in this, the requirement stands as an announcement of the commitment of the state and a declaration of its norms.

A vehicle of language is also needed to describe the nature of different religious groups and their attitudes towards the wider society. Sociologists of religion have elaborated many typologies of religious organizations since Weber and Troeltsch first drew attention to the distinction between

In the West!

More than an Han: 1960!

church-type and sect-type Christianity, but their original distinctions still help to define the poles of the argument.[1]

The *church-type* organization, laying stress on the institutional character of the church, defines its life in relationship to its priesthood and the ministry of word and sacrament. Since the focus of its activity lies here it may appear reluctant to give precise definition to its membership, other than by reference to infant baptism, for ideally it champions the identity of the religious community with society at large. Its concern is therefore with all men, and not confined to the elect. Moreover, since its holiness is assured by priesthood and sacraments, it has found itself able to co-operate with the secular order without any sense of contamination, and indeed it has normally sought a close relationship with the state in terms of patronage and establishment. At the local level it manifests itself in parish responsibility rather than church fellowship. Whereas within the Catholic tradition such a concept of church transcends national boundaries, within Protestantism it has more often operated within and been allied to specific nationalities.

The *sect-type*, by contrast, defines the church not from a priesthood and hierarchy downwards but from the belief and commitment of the individual believer upwards. It represents the church as gathered out of society, and set under the law of Christ. By contrast with the church-type, membership is precise and discipline is rigorous and indeed its concern for purity of membership may provoke a pietistic rejection of all forms of responsibility for the wider society, and an attempt to establish a separate Christian society within society at large.

These two patterns should not be seen as exclusive definitions but as part either of a spectrum of ecclesiastical stances or better of an essential dialectic within religious experience.

Later sociologists of religion, and more particularly H. Richard Niebuhr in *The Social Sources of Denominationalism* (New York, 1929), have added to this base the language of *denomination* to explain both the institutionalization of some sect-type organizations and the accommodation of some church-type hierarchies to a *de facto* pluralism of belief and organization. The denomination, in contrast to the sect, accepts the need for a working relationship with existing political institutions, is less pessimistic

1. Troeltsch, *The Social Teaching of the Christian Churches* (1911; English Translation, 2 vols., London, 1931).

about human history, and is encumbered by a weightier institutional machine. The process of evolution from sect to denomination has been widely discussed whereas the corresponding evolution towards denomination from church origins has been less fully documented. The process is nevertheless apparent as church-type organizations have had to come to terms with the breaking down of unitary cultures. Apart from other considerations, in the processes of history all pretence to exclusive representation of religious belief has had to be surrendered as alternative forms of Christian commitment have been recognized as in some way valid. Accordingly the concept of denomination assumes no exclusive claims but rather stands for a 'pluralistic legitimacy' as each group comes to play down competition and recognize at least the partial legitimacy of its rivals. Church-type and sect-type religious organizations may, though not necessarily so, coalesce in the newer pattern of denominational life which in itself is evidence of the pluralism of Christian experience that exists in the state.

Idea of Christendom

So much for definitions and abstractions. Historically the story must start with the emergence of Christendom. The idea of Christendom was one of power and territory, an attempt at a geographical incarnation of the gospel. In fact Christendom dated back to Constantine's first steps towards the establishment of Christianity as the religion of the Roman Empire in A.D. 313, but its development owed quite as much to the threat presented by the rapid advance of Islam in the south in the years following the prophet's death in A.D. 632 as earlier it had benefitted from the threat of successive attacks of barbarians in the north. In other words the emergence of the concept of Christendom was in large measure a response to fears of incipient pluralism: it represents a backs-to-the-wall defence of inherited culture and virtues savagely under attack from external forces. That the threat could as well be internal is witnessed to by the history of the medieval church's attitudes to heresy: a crusade against the Albigenses in Southern France was as much a defence of Christendom as was an attack upon the infidel in the Holy Land, for heresy represented not merely theological deviancy but a threat upon the stability of an indivisible

Christendom. Church and state were coterminous: baptism signified entrance not only into the ecclesiastical community but into the civil community as well. That is to say, behind the idea of Christendom lay the medieval principle of totality. 'The atomization of our activities into religious, political, moral, cultural, economic and other spheres' was alien to this world of Christendom; rather 'man was whole and indivisible', every one of his actions amenable to judgement by Christian norms and standards, norms and standards established and motivated by the church authority. This was the import, according to the medieval papacy, of Christ's words to Peter, 'Whatever you bind on earth shall be bound in heaven' (Matt. 16:19). This was quite unambiguous in its all-embracing scope and stamp: 'whatever' meant whatever, nothing was excluded, and heavenly action consequent on judgements in this world meant that these were final judgements against which there could be no appeal.[2]

Notice what we are discussing: it is the claim upon obedience made by Christendom and its papal directors. We know that from time to time groups of men rebelled against this Catholic totalitarianism; we know that in many respects the Christian culture of medieval Europe was only skin-deep, and that it compromised with an ongoing paganism, not to mention its Islamic neighours and a resurgent Hellenism. All this is admitted. But the theory remains as a testimony to political intention and ambition, to what the state would have liked to secure, if only it had the power: not merely a unitary state but a unitary Christian domain (for that is what 'Christendom' means), at least in western Europe.

Collapse of Christendom

But right from the moment of its creation, this Christendom was a fragile institution and suffered numerous set-backs: the schism of eastern and western Christendom in 1054, a constant pattern of strife and petty war amongst the western kingdoms, but above all the threat of the Ottoman Turk on the eastern frontier. In this respect what came to be most important for the idea of Christendom was that some Christian powers were prepared to make alliances with the Turk against their Christian neighbours. The rise of Islam had initially for-

2. W. Ullmann, *Principles of Government and Politics in the Middle Ages* (London, 1961), pp. 32-36.

tified the idea of Christendom but the westward thrust of the
Islamic Ottomans in the fifteenth century well-nigh broke it.
In the context of such action Christendom was made a
vacuous word: Erasmus appealed to 'the nations of Europe',
not the members of Christendom, to crusade against the
Turk. Even without the Reformation the transition from the
religious 'Christendom' to the secular 'Europe' was already
in progress.[3]

Hard upon competing nations however, came competing
sects, but even before that with William of Ockham and the
fourteenth-century nominalists the Thomist synthesis between revelation and reason was under attack, in favour of the
discrete study of theology and philosophy as separate and
autonomous spheres of intellectual activity. Even as the
political unity of the Christian west was constantly menaced
by diverging interests so the old unity of thought was under
threat a century or more before the Reformation.

The breach between the Reformers and the papacy was
not as simple as the schism four centuries earlier between
Rome and Constantinople, for the attempts at pan-
Protestantism failed and the division in the church that
occurred was multiple rather than simple. Moreover a combination of the rising nationalism of sixteenth-century
Europe and the essential conservatism of the Reformers,
meant that national Protestant churches, *Volkskirchen* or
Landeskirchen, embracing the old caesaro-papism of the Middle Ages, became the order of the day. The territorial principle of the Peace of Augsburg (1555) — *cuius regio, eius
religio*: the religion of a territory shall be the religion of the
prince who rules it — combined with a deep religious respect
for the rule of the magistracy, whether territorial prince or
city oligarchy, meant that plurality developed between territories rather than within territories. Something of the men-
tality of Christendom lingered on in these separate states
where the Reformers still maintained the old equation of
church and state and where theological judgement still
dominated everyday life. On the one hand, princely resort to
the idea of the divine right of kings witnessed both the continued application of medieval theology to political affairs,
and the overlapping jurisdictions of church and state; on the
other, a religious justification of revolution was deemed
essential to the politics of opposition, for no-one wanted

3. P. Coles, *The Ottoman Impact on Europe* (New York, 1968), p. 148.

both God and the king as their enemies.

Indeed it was just because the Anabaptists opposed the identity of church and state in what they called 'everybody's church' that they were so bitterly persecuted. Their emergence, therefore, highlights part of the dialectic of ecclesiology described by Troeltsch: the alternatives of parish- or church-type Christianity, on the one hand, and sect-type Christianity on the other. Where the Anabaptists survived the hostility alike of papal and reformed antagonists, they, with their commitment to a church of believers only, added to the pluralism of religious choice, in much the same way as the separatists were later to do in England.

Birth of Secularism

In such a context of choice, then, the lay and secular spirit of the renaissance flourished. Many commentators noted the secularizing of mental interests at a time when dogmatic differences occasioned so much bloodshed: Sir Thomas Browne thought his experience was like that of an amphibian as he found himself consciously required to adjust to existing in more than one intellectual element. All thinking men, in professor Dickens's words, 'found themselves in a world which had made itself far more independent of Christian controls than the world of the late Middle Ages'.[4] So with the Reformation the intellectual climate changed.

New stress was laid by this process upon the free choice made by the individual. Society was at once atomized and secularized. The sovereignty of individual conscience, though doubtless it deepened the religious intensity of the life of the church, also secularized the life of society. So it has been said, 'Christian conscience was the force which began to make Europe "secular",'[5] even as it was pious men who claimed that religious experience must be personal, who first shattered the old dream of one universal Christian society.[6]

In this pluralist climate it is perhaps significant that some

4. A. G. Dickens, *Reformation and Society in Sixteenth-Century Europe* (London, 1966), pp. 196-197.
5. O. Chadwick, *The Secularization of the European Mind in the Ninteenth Century* (Cambridge, 1975), p. 23.
6. See H. Butterfield, 'Reflections on Religion and Modern Individualism', in J. A. Burrell, ed., *The Role of Religion in Modern European History* (New York, 1964), p. 142.

Christian groups developed voluntarist forms of church association. Rejecting parish Christianity, they conceived of the church as a free assemblage of committed believers, called out of the world into spiritual fellowship. The old social solidarity was gone: a man was born into the state but needed to be reborn into the church. Their ethics were in large measure community ethics rather than social ethics; their own communities they governed by the rule of love whilst in society at large they exhibited a general suspicion of all magisterial action. In matters of faith most certainly no coercion was appropriate, for only Christ himself could be 'the key and language of the church and the conscience'. If the law was impotent to secure uniformity, then toleration became a necessity.

Growth of Toleration

But such early pleas for religious toleration were not widely acclaimed. At a time when the English Presbyterians denounced toleration as 'the Devil's masterpiece', Cromwell's image suffered more from his religious magnanimity at home than from the penal rigour of his Irish administration abroad. At the Restoration, with the bitter experience of religious war high in its memory, the restored Church of England was faced with having to decide between two policies, comprehension and toleration. Those favouring comprehension argued that some small adjustment of Anglican doctrine, and more particularly of Anglican practice, would accommodate the vast majority of dissenters and leave only the fanatics outside the state church, thereby managing to salvage the idea of the Church of England as indeed the church of the English nation. But this was not to be: the opposition of the High Church Party ensured that it was the alternative policy of toleration of tender consciences that was eventually implemented in 1689. This had dire consequences for the position of the established church when it was discovered that freedom to attend conventicles could also be interpreted as freedom not to attend church at all. Toleration of tender consciences in the event involved also toleration of apathetic consciences and therefore marked an important stage in the development of a society in which religious belief was emphasized as arising out of a judgement both private and voluntary. That is the problem with the idea of toleration: as Owen Chadwick expressed it, 'From the moment that European opinion decided for toleration, it decided for an eventual free market in opinion. A toleration of a minority is not the same as equality before the law between opinions. But in the circumstances of European history the one must lead into the other . . . A free market in some opinions became a free market in all opinions.'[7] If we are tempted in our day to seek to reimpose a Christendom ideal on our society then it needs to be noted that a last desperate attempt to maintain a unitary state in Britain, by way of reordering the state church on more comprehensive lines, failed to find favour both in the late seventeenth century and also in the 1830s when Thomas Arnold renewed this kind of programme of church reform.

From the Act of Toleration onwards an implicit pluralism, at least of varieties of Protestant allegiance, in some measure characterized British life. The nineteenth century saw the continuation and even the acceleration of this process. With the repeal of the Test and Corporation Acts in 1828 the Anglican constitution came to an end and with Catholic Emancipation in the following year the Protestant constitution. The word 'secularist' was first used in 1851 and by 1886 the right of an unbeliever to sit in parliament had been conceded. Formally, and exclusively, the Christian constitution of England was at an end, though informally and influentially Christian paramountcy continued to dominate the affairs of state. But perhaps more important than formal changes was a change in interest, for as Professor Marsh has shown, at just this time parliament showed itself more and more reluctant to give time to ecclesiastical business, which was unfortunate in so far as the church had a great need for ongoing reform. Matters of state now took priority over matters of church establishment.[8]

Nineteenth-Century Pluralism

Not only the pace of change in the nineteenth century but also its range and scope should be held firmly in mind. Professor Chadwick makes this same point when he affirms, 'The problem of secularization is not the same as the problem of enlightenment. Enlightenment was of the few. Seculariza-

7. Chadwick, *op. cit.*, p. 21.
8. P. T. Marsh, *The Victorian Church in Decline: Archbishop Tait and the Church of England, 1868-82* (London, 1969).

tion is of the many.'[9] And whereas the men of the early
enlightenment lived within a calendar of sunrise and sunset,
sowing and harvest, of the seasons in their order, a world
where providential explanations of experience were widely
accepted, the contrived world of industry and capital, of
mechanical time and of urban communities divorced from a
direct sense of dependence on the land, had quite a different
impact on the popular mind. Instead of the mystery of the
divine ordering of events, there arose a brash confidence in
human design and accomplishment. So the pluralism of belief
that emerges after the crises of 1828/9 is of a wholly different
order from that which had been tolerated in the previous one
hundred and fifty years. The issue now was not merely the
pluralism of a variety of forms of Christian belief and
practice, but a pluralism of belief and unbelief, a pluralism
that witnessed the emergence of overt secularism, evolutionary history and sociology, and Marxist Socialism, all of
them the more powerful because of the broadcasting capacities of a rising press which embraced an ever-widening
literate or semi-literate public as the century drew to a close.

In this process, another aspect of pluralism needs to be
noted. In an earlier age the pulpit had, as one Victorian
preacher expressed it, been 'newspaper, schoolmaster, theological treatise, a stimulant to good works, historical lecture,
metaphysics etc. all in one'.[10] But no longer was this so. The
clerisy could no longer be assumed to be wholly Christian. In
the marketplace of communications Christian proclamation
had to compete with a multitude of voices, committed and
uncommitted. The church no longer shaped the public mind,
but rather found itself responding to stimuli from a hundred
other areas of human experience. In particular it is important
to take note that this growth of pluralism occurs alongside a
revolutionary growth in the activities of the state and its
increasing appetite to control more and more of the lives of
its citizens. And when the state reflects the plurality of belief
and non-belief of its members, then its influence, though
hopefully making for justice and even mercy, must necessarily emphasize the secular nature of life in the modern
world. That the true character of these changes has often
been masked and improperly appreciated does not deny the
reality of their existence.

9. Chadwick, *op. cit.*, p. 9.
10. F. W. Robertson, cited by Horton Davies, *Worship and Theology in England*,
vol. 4: *From Newman to Martineau, 1850-1900* (Princeton, 1962), p. 282.

For example, it has often been argued that the Christian, and more particularly the evangelical conscience, exercised a deliberate and powerful influence on the life of Victorian England, but a more penetrating analysis may suggest that this appears to be the case only because there was a prior invasion of the theological mind by the secular philosophy of individualism. Indeed it now seems clear that whilst this skewing of the Christian conscience in an individualist, even laissez-faire direction, led to an emphasis upon a number of moralistic crusades, it co-existed with the toleration of a number of great social abuses: the dehumanizing structures of the textile and sweated industries, the oppression of women in society, and the prosecution of opium wars in the imperial interest, to name but three examples.

In the world of the mind, providential explanation of human experience had to face competitive mechanistic explanations. Although not always taken to be denials of providence such explanations still offered alternative accounts of human behaviour, especially when the biological phase of the science-and-religion debate led on to the sociological and psychological. Everywhere there was a movement away from the ultimate to the immediate. The best logical analyses certainly recognized that there was no inherent conflict here, but concern for one as over against the other indicates a crucial change of intellectual climate. For example, in international relations there was a new emphasis upon sheer expediency and the dynamics of power. There emerges a more nakedly secular viewpoint, unconcerned about all doctrines and metaphysics. Functionalism rather than allegiance to principle was all that mattered: old fashioned journalists at the time of the Franco-Prussian War regretted the passing of the old international moral order (perhaps a last legacy of old Christendom) in favour of *realpolitik*, though it should be noted at the same time that the very destructiveness of modern warfare, even within a secular environment, has given rise, albeit falteringly, to a new search for international order.

Part of the dilemma for the church in this changing situation was that she too easily became identified with an unthinking conservatism. English Evangelicals may not have produced any statement as comprehensive in its condemnation of modern civilization as the Papal Syllabus of Errors of 1864, but their suspicious response to a changing world could sometimes be little less negative. This intellectual conservatism was often accompanied by a social conservatism, a too close and uncritical identification with the static part of the social structure of the age.

Dilemma of the Church of England

In this respect the Church of England faced a particular problem in so far as she had become fully integrated into the life of the aristocractic England of the eighteenth century: religious conformity in consequence both 'symbolized and reinforced the cohesion of an established social order'.[11] When the processes of industrialization began to corrode that stability, the church's identification with the old order meant that she no longer fulfilled a universal integrative function but now a partisan and privileged one. The changes in society associated with industrialization were far-reaching in their implications, involving changes in economic organization, social thinking and political representation which were not easily worked out in the context of the widespread fears begotten of the French Revolution. The challenges were not altogether new, as any familiarity with the history of the seventeenth century would indicate. Pluralistic society in England was already partly developed, but there was a new sense of crisis and foreboding, a sense of the almost total dislocation of the traditional society. The temptation for the Church of England was to engage in a yet more thorough reliance upon its established position and this in part accounts for the worsening of relationships with dissent at this time. But the Church could not stop the new society from coming into being, and that new society was a plural society in which there was a diversity of wealth, commercial as well as landed, and a diversity of classes all with their differing cultural aspirations. The old coherence was shattered. No longer could it even theoretically be argued that all men belonged together in one monopolistic culture of deference and responsibility. You see this clearly in political terms: the apologetic for an unreformed House of Commons was that there was a coherence within the different interests in society and that whilst those interests were *actually* represented, the people were *virtually* represented by their social superiors.

11. A. D. Gilbert, *Religion and Society in Industrial England: Church, Chapel and Social Change, 1740-1914* (London, 1976), p. 75.

But when men began to be conscious of a horizontal solidarity with men of a similar class, and when they began to see their superiors, either landlords or employers, as opposing rather than representing their interests, then the theory became obsolete. It is, in some measure, this recognition of the tensions that existed in the older patterns of social organization, this recognition of the emergence of class as a dominant social discipline, that lies behind the passing of the Reform Bill in 1832. This was the new social reality with which the churches had to come to grips.

Accordingly because the social reality had changed, the maintenance of a church-type organization by the Church of England had to be reconsidered. In response to social as well as religious fragmentation the Church of England in the nineteenth century assumed a denominational outlook. The other denominations were recognized and a co-operative pattern of co-existence was evolved, whilst at local level, the church, though not relinquishing parochial claims, became increasingly congregational, again particularly as it responded to the growth of conflicting parties within its own church order. Whilst formal disestablishment did not follow, much accommodation of other Christian bodies, not to mention secular influences, did. Exclusive control over the registering and sanctifying of the processes of 'hatching, matching and despatching' came to an end, as did the responsibility for the maintenance of church buildings by the population at large, and the established Church's monopoly of higher education. Fierce battles were fought over church education. The monarchy remained loyally and effectively Anglican and most of the bishops remained in the House of Lords on the basis of a formula worked out in the nineteenth century. In the twentieth century the 'pluralistic legitimacy' of all mainstream Christian sects has been recognized in a number of areas, as for example in hospital and military chaplaincies and religious broadcasting, whilst indirectly a great deal of state money has been made available to churches of all denominations.

Twentieth Century

Nevertheless, the spread of secularization has continued unabated, aided by disillusion with the shallow liberal optimism brought about by two world wars. Even without reference to migration factors, the revolution in communications has set the life of our nation in a context of world religious belief and political commitments, making impossible any thought of an insular or merely British solution to our problem. Migration has added to the phenomenon of plurality as large communities of members of other living faiths have established religious communities in this country, whilst the historic churches have shown themselves less than expert in drawing Christians of other ethnic origins into the worshipping and witnessing community.

All this is true, but it is equally true that even in the twentieth century we still live with the inheritance of Christendom, and the crucial issue for our development of social ethics is to decide whether our strategy should be to attempt to renovate the idea of Christendom, or rather, not merely reluctantly, but gladly to accept the nature of our modern secular society and to try within its context to discover an appropriate mode for expressing our discipleship.

Within the Church of England in the early 1920s there emerged the Christendom Group of Catholic social thought that published the series of essays entitled *The Return of Christendom* in 1922 and, after the Second World War, a second symposium entitled *Prospect for Christendom* (1945).[12] In many respects their thinking embraced some of the most creative work then accomplished in Christian social ethics which is still worthy of serious consideration today. But the language of their title represents a nostalgia that dates their work to a bygone age. The 1944 Education Act perpetuated the same obsolescence: though worked out in a context in which only a minority of the population were practising Christians it put the Christian faith in a privileged position as the officially recognized 'stance for living' inherited from the centuries of the 'Christendom era'.

The Modern Debate

The best plea for Christendom-type thinking in the modern world is to be found in T. S. Eliot's *The Idea of a Christian Society* which dates to the eve of the outbreak of the Second

---

12. *The Return of Christendom*, by a group of Churchmen, with an introduction by C. Gore and an epilogue by G. K. Chesterton (London, 1922); M. B. Reckitt (ed.) *Prospect for Christendom: Essays in Catholic Social Reconstruction* (London, 1945).

World War. Viewing a Europe split between materialistic fascism and materialistic communism Eliot sensed that the mass of English people still held an undisplayed commitment to Christianity. He deduced that in the moment of crisis they would reject the 'neutral society' of the politicians in favour of something more distinctively Christian. His own belief was 'that the only alternative to a progressive and insidious adaptation to totalitarian worldliness for which the pace is already set, is to aim at a Christian society'. Such a society would possess three elements: the Christian state or legislative aspect; the Christian community, the vast mass of people who conformed 'largely unconsciously' to Christian norms of behaviour; and finally the community of Christians from whom alone could one expect 'a conscious Christian life in its highest social level'. In such a context he argues against disestablishment: 'The effect on the mind of the people of the visible and dramatic withdrawal of the Church from the affairs of the nation, of the deliberate recognition of two standards and ways of life, of the Church's abandonment of all those who are not by their wholehearted profession within the fold — this is incalculable . . . . I am convinced that you cannot have a national Christian society, a religious-social community, a society with a political philosophy founded upon the Christian faith, if it is constituted as a mere congeries of private and independent sects. The national faith must have an official recognition by the State, as well as accepted status in the community and a basis of conviction in the heart of the individual.'[13] Eliot's plea is a curious one because whilst it admits a declension from Christian belief and commitments, it still hopes to maintain allegiance to Christian norms. This is what makes it adopt ambiguous Coleridgian language to describe non-believing 'Christian' citizens. In the context of the Europe of 1939 that was perhaps a reasonable plea, but this analysis seems to offer little illumination for society in our own day. One would not want to argue with Eliot's wide vision of appropriate Christian concern, and it seems to me that an emphasis on striving towards the establishment of the kingdom of God must always correct any tendency to limit or privatize the areas of religious concern in a pluralist society. The issue with which we have to grapple, however, concerns the use of the power of the state and the nature of the religious justification of

13. *The Idea of a Christian Society* (London, 1939), pp. 20-21, 26-28, 49-51.

this. By what rights may the Christian conscience impose Christian norms on the uncommitted and those of other faiths? Were the boundaries of church and state once more coterminous, would it be right to use the power of the state to secure the Christian morality of all citizens? What is the relationship between a pattern of life freely chosen and that same pattern of life implemented as a response to the state's demand?

Moreover it is important that we do not become too parochial in our judgement about pluralism. Though recognition of our pluralist situation in Great Britain may involve a painful recognition for many of us, in the United States the fact of plurality of belief led from the very beginning of the federation to a separation of church and state, and her subsequent history has shown that this has certainly not meant that Christian believers have been prevented from bringing their consciences to bear on political issues. In this, of course, Christian statesmen have been assisted by the fact that although the state may be secular, society or its members appear to continue to be profoundly religious, which properly alerts us to the distinction between state and society. At the end of the last century Lord Bryce observed that 'so far from suffering from want of State support, religion seemed in the United States to stand all the firmer because, standing alone, she is seen to stand by her own strength'.[14]

It must, moreover, be recognized that it has been a gain to Christian missionaries in many places for the apparatus of government to recognize the pluralism of belief within their territories (e.g. India, Japan, Indonesia). Furthermore the problem of church-state relations in eastern Europe has to do with securing a greater recognition of the implications of a pluralism of commitments. In many respects, the situation there may be represented as a mirror image of the conventional situation in the west: namely the commitment of the state to a particular doctrinal stance, albeit one of political doctrine, which does less than justice to the plurality of commitments within the society concerned. It is difficult, to say the least, to argue for a recognition of pluralism abroad, as the evangelical conscience has so often done, and to refuse to face the implications of its dominance of our own domestic life.

In 1962, D. L. Munby replied to Eliot with *The Idea of a*

---

14. Cited by D. Edwards, *Religion and Change* (London, 1969), p. 92.

Secular Society in which he made a plea for Christians to
have done with patching up the old idea of Christendom and
instead by conscious commitment not only to recognize the
secular nature of society but even to rejoice in it as the creation of western Christianity,[15] claiming it as a society 'framed
more nearly in accordance with the Will of God as seen in
Scripture, in the Incarnation and in the way God actually
treats men, than those societies which have attempted to impose on the mass of men what a small Christian group have
believed to be in accordance with God's Will'.[16] Though his
language is not always as clear as it might be, the advantages
of the secular state are strikingly spelt out by Munby:

> The Christian claim differs from that of the pure secularist, not
> in a belief that the secularist has failed to understand one part of
> life — religion, nor in a necessarily different moral code in
> everyday matters. It differs in the belief in God, who exists
> behind the world and on whom it depends. The secular world
> has its limited aims, and God respects these; there are no other
> alternative aims for Christians in their everyday life. But Chris-
> tians, believing in God, can see these aims as *limited,* precisely
> because they look for *ultimate* satisfaction to God alone.[17]

The kind of emphasis that Munby made was expressed even
more forcefully three years later in Harvey Cox's *The Secular
City*. The exaggerations of his position have been properly
criticized, but the general tenor of his argument has been
widely influential. In particular, for our purposes, we may
note that Cox made an important distinction between secularization and secularism. Secularization implies an historical
process, almost certainly irreversible, in which society and
culture are delivered from tutelage to religious control and
closed metaphysical world views. Secularism, on the other
hand is the name for an ideology, a new closed world-view
which functions very much like a new religion. While secularization finds its roots in the biblical faith in western history,
this is not the case with secularism. Like any other 'ism', it
menaces the openness and freedom secularization has produced; it must therefore be watched carefully to prevent it
becoming the ideology of a new establishment.[18]

15. D. L. Munby, *The Idea of a Secular Society* (Oxford, 1963).
16. *Ibid.* p. 34.
17. *Ibid.* p. 76.
18. H. Cox, *The Secular City* (London, 1965), pp. 20-21.

Education

The increasing realization of the secular context of contemporary experience will have particular repercussions at many points. Paul Hirst tries to relate the kind of things that Munby and Cox are saying to the area of moral education. He claims that a credal approach to moral education is not appropriate to our modern pluralist position and tries to put forward as an alternative the position of what he calls 'secular Christians' — those who 'would claim that the true character of their religious beliefs only emerges when they are combined with a thorough secularization of all other areas of human thought and experience'.[19] And for Hirst morality and education both represent 'other areas of human thought and experience'. First with regard to education, 'the idea that there is a characteristically or distinctively Christian form of education seems just as much a mistake as the idea that there is a distinctively Christian form of mathematics, of engineering or of farming'.[20] He further argues that to assert the significance of moral and scientific knowledge in the Christian world view does not entail saying that such knowledge must have a religious justification. Even as Christians over the centuries have reconciled themselves to accepting the 'independence of science from religion as central to Christian teaching, an expression of the mandate that God has given to man as called on to "subdue the earth" ', so now they must also come to accept the view that in the moral sphere man has a similar autonomy, and again it is argued that 'Christian belief rightly understood necessitates this' as in line with biblical teaching about natural morality.[21] He concludes that Christian teaching can never hope to be coherent if it denies the legitimacy of living in secular terms: 'What it has to do is to get clear the place of this form of life within a Christian perspective'.[22]

Morality and Law

Another area of lively debate that has been linked to the process of secularization but arising from quite different sources, is that of the relationship between morality and the law.

19. P. H. Hirst, *Moral Education in a Secular Society* (London, 1974), p. 3.
20. *Ibid.* p. 77.
21. *Ibid.* pp. 22-23.
22. *Ibid.* p. 27.

The *Wolfenden Report of the Committee on Homosexual Offences and Prostitution*, published in 1957, in debating the scope and function of the criminal law in relationship to sexual ethics provoked considerable response. In answer to the question, 'What constitutes a crime?' Wolfenden gave a positive and a negative definition: the criminal law had a responsibility 'to preserve public order and decency, to protect the citizen from what is offensive or injurious, and to provide sufficient safeguards against exploitation and corruption by others, particularly those who are specially vulnerable because they are young, weak in body or mind, inexperienced, or in a state of special physical, official or economic dependence'.[23] By contrast, the Committee following the general principles of John Stuart Mill's classic defence of individual liberties, argued: 'It is not, in our view, the function of the law to intervene in the private lives of citizens, or to seek to enforce any particular pattern of behaviour . . .'[24] The document goes on to argue that it cannot be held that the law should cover all forms of sexual behaviour even though many might object to certain practices in these areas: 'certain forms of sexual behaviour are regarded by many as sinful, morally wrong or objectionable for reasons of conscience, or of religious or cultural tradition; and such actions may be reprobated on these grounds'.[25] But this was not a sufficient argument for making them criminal. The report argues later that 'There must remain a realm of private morality and immorality which is in brief and crude terms, not the law's business'.[26]

Lord Devlin in *The Enforcement of Morals* (1959) challenged Wolfenden's distinction between the public and the private both as a matter of fact and as a matter of desirability. Euthanasia might be cited as an example of the law's invasion of the area of the private as a matter of fact, and Devlin argued that this involvement of the law in the private lives of individuals was properly done since a society is bound together not merely by a political system but by a common morality. 'The suppression of vice is as much the law's business as the suppression of subversive activities; it is no more possible to define a sphere of private morality than it

23. *Report of the Committee on Homosexual Offences and Prostitution (The Wolfenden Report,* London, 1957), pp. 9-10.
24. *Ibid.* p. 10.
25. *Ibid.*
26. *Ibid.* p. 24.

is to define one of private subversive activity.'[27]

Devlin's argument is essentially that a society has a right, which certainly it should employ sparingly, to use the instrument of law to defend itself by securing minimum standards of behaviour from its members. This position has been challenged by Professor H. L. A. Hart in his *Law, Liberty and Morality* who argues that Devlin's contention, that the preservation of a society's morality is essential to its continued existence, is an argument 'unsupported by evidence' which is also based on the wrongful assumption 'that all sexual morality together with the morality that forbids acts injurious to others such as killing, stealing and dishonesty — forms a single seamless web, so that those who deviate from any part are likely or perhaps bound to deviate from the whole'.[28]

Recognizing then that Devlin's position is not without its critics, we should notice that even on his argument the actual condition of society, and the desire to protect it, are the criterion by which the enforcement of morality is to be judged, that is, the nature of society takes precedence over legal disciplines. In this respect a plural society will produce laws which recognize the plural nature of that society, and therefore it is to the nature of society that the Christian conscience ought in the first instance to give its attention. If the morality that the law has a right to enforce is to be a reflection of the condition of society and its culture, then Christian social responsibility must involve an attempt to influence that society to give proper respect to true human values. It may be that in some areas there needs to be a new attempt to secure a higher social consensus more respectful of true human dignity, before we can hope to proceed to legislative action. At the very least our ethical concerns ought to be worked out in actions which are culturally persuasive as well as legislatively coercive. This will necessarily involve an attempt to find some common ground for sharing with others, who, though having different beliefs from ours, nevertheless have a similar concern for the moral order of both state and society. Professor Anderson has suggested that there are valid arguments, even outside Scripture, which demonstrate that the basic moral teaching which Christians accept as part of the biblical revelation, represents what is most beneficial

---

27. P. A. Devlin, *The Enforcement of Morals* (London, 1959), pp. 13-14.
28. H. L. A. Hart, *Law, Liberty and Morality* (London, 1963), pp. 50-51.

for man's life in society, and argues that it 'is on such grounds that this teaching and, where appropriate, legislation based on it, can be commended to non-Christians in a pluralistic democracy'.[29] It is to this task that we have to address ourselves.

As yet, however, the issues are not well-focused. There exists a lack of confidence among Christians, torn between the familiar world they know and the world that is emerging all around them, as to what their attitude and commitments should be. In particular they must learn to distinguish clearly between what is the legacy of history and what is the biblical pattern of thinking.

why?
This is
a very dangerous argument

Jesus and the Pluralist Society

Jesus and the apostles were not defended by any rules of establishment. Theirs was not a protected position. Their moral concern for society as also their evangelism proceeded from a position of no social esteem. The teaching that Jesus gave his disciples was accordingly directly related to the problems of living in a pluralistic society of competing creeds and beliefs. What then was the basis for their working out an approach to the moral problems of their day? In the first place the disciples were called to affirm the goodness of creation. The created world and human society represent a divine creation providentially upheld by God's power. Because it is his creation, it must never cease to be our concern. In this world the disciples are called to uphold the uncompromising demands of God's justice and righteousness. These need to be reflected in our day-to-day relationships in human society. The call here is not merely negative, for Jesus adds to the proper prophetic fury the compassionate call to his followers to discover the true meaning of being a neighbour. The disciples are called to establish the kingdom with all the pervasiveness of the image of salt: their witness is to be in the world and not apart from it. It is in fact God himself who establishes his kingdom but they are to look for its coming. Accordingly the relationship between kingdom and church is one of crucial poignancy for the present discussion on social ethics. The Bible also clearly witnesses to the widespread sovereignty of sin as imprisoning not only individuals but institutions, but

29. J. N. D. Anderson, *Morality, Law and Grace* (London, 1972), p. 82.

affirms that the rebellious powers of this world have been brought into captivity by the cross and there they must stay, even though they still essay to organize and corrupt even the best human aspirations. Finally, amidst all the tangle of this-worldly relationships the Christian is called to affirm that history is not purposeless but moves towards the fulfilment of the new creation when the whole universe, not simply rebellious men, will be reconciled to Christ as Head.

Agenda for Christians

Christians today have to come to a judgement about the nature of the society in which they live: do they in fact live in a pluralist society or is this a false description? On the basis of this judgement they must decide upon the mode of their own Christian citizenship. Is the renovation of the Christendom idea a viable option? Is society sufficiently Christian to allow the imposition of Christian norms on the whole population? Does the Christendom view treat the actual social situation sufficiently realistically or is its vision distorted by an out-dated optimism about the Christian permeation of society? Is a Christian community free to enforce Christian standards on non-believers or is there a Christian conscience on the extent to which the coercive power of the state can properly be employed to such an end? Would it be possible, even among Christians, to secure a sufficient consensus to establish a programme of definite and deliberate action? Alternatively an analysis of the present social situation might be taken to argue for a pietistic withdrawal from the world as hopelessly given over to sin. Because, it might be argued, there is no hope for the world at large, Christians must seek radical remedies and seek to establish a society within a society, and take up a position within the ascetic tradition of the church along with medieval monks and sixteenth-century Anabaptists. To many of us to act in such a way would be to act with unjustified pessimism about God's work in the world and to surrender the common life of society into the hands of materialist agencies. Again such action would also tend to represent a fragmentation of the Christian body into a number of self-concerned ghetto groups as much in conflict with each other as the world.

The nature of society may be pluralist and the outlook of the state may be secular but there is a style of active Christian citizenship that can be worked out even in this context. To accept the pluralist nature of society, and to be reluctant to seek special privileges of the secular state, does not confine the Christian citizen to a role of passivity or neutrality. Though without rights or power to impose conformity of belief or practice on his fellow citizens, he will feel free to struggle to commend and implement strategies and policies, informed and inspired by the biblical view of man, of human welfare and of justice in society, with all the energy and passion that he can command, freely arguing with those of differing persuasions, giving their views the same respect that he can legitimately expect for his own. The call to active involvement and to passionate campaign exists independently of the nature of both society and state, though its implementation will obviously depend upon the context.

Reading List

P. Abrecht, *The Churches and Rapid Social Change* (London, 1961).
B. Mitchell, *Law, Morality and Religion in a Secular Society* (London, 1967).
L. Newbigin, *Christian Witness in a Plural Society* (London, 1977).
D. Sheppard, *Built as a City: God and the Urban World Today* (London, 1974).
Other works are listed in the text and the notes.

Questions for Discussion

1   Does the advent of the pluralist state require us to be morally neutral and to suspend Christian commitment in political life?

2   Relate the law-making responsibilities of Christian majorities to the position of Christian minorities (e.g. the stance adopted by Christians in the west to the position encountered by Christian minorities in e.g. an Islamic state or eastern Europe).

3   What are the implications of living in a pluralist society for (a) moral education and (b) the law of the family?

4   What part has legislation to play in the building up of a sense of community in an ethnically diverse society? Does an acceptance of pluralism deny the need to work for integration?

5   Is it time to have done with attempts at renovating the idea of Christendom and for a new and deliberate search to be undertaken to discover an appropriate mode for Christians to 'do politics' in a pluralist state?

Chapter Four
Towards a Theology of the State
Haddon Willmer

Towards a Theology of the State

THE MOST IMPORTANT WORD IN MY TITLE IS 'TOWARDS'. I do not come to you as an expert with the answers. I am a theologian *in via*, on the road, because the theologian can never be more than a man and a Christian. Seeing through a glass darkly is therefore natural to him. Christian existence is not different from human and political existence in this respect: in both church and state human communities are always going forward into the unknown, unprescribed yet not unconditioned future as it becomes present. Our position as theologians does not differ from our positions as people and as Christians. It is not as though we have an assured theology and on that basis move towards maturity and effectiveness as persons; we are always working towards a satisfactory theology, with a faith seeking understanding. *Semper reformanda* applies as much to the thinking, the theology of the church, as to its order and actions.

This paper is a thought-experiment and confession of faith together. Many Evangelicals have little time for theology as thought-experiment. They are competent and courageous in other specialisms and so they prove in practice the indispensability of experiment and imagination. But in theology it is different. Safety first — and last — pinions the wings of the mind, for imagination is of the devil. So either they do without theology altogether or they claim to be in possession of it, by inheritance, without working very hard for it. Theology cannot be made so neat and easy. It is too close to prayer and speculation and fantasy, too vulnerable to self-examination, and to life, for tidiness. It becomes, as liberation theologians say, reflection on practice, though in a broader way than they conceive. We can only manage to be really theologians if we are naturally reckless or we believe in God over and above all our theologizings, or both, like Karl Barth or G. K. Chesterton.[1]

Besides the character of theology, there is another reason for this 'towards', which is specific to the subject of the state. In social ethics and in practice we have to deal with the state as it is today and as it might be tomorrow. The Roman Empire of the first century and the kingdom of Solomon are not the subject of Christian social ethics, however educative reflection on them might be. We cannot take over a theology or ethic developed in relation to those states, without testing the assumption that the state as we have it today is of the same species. Of course there are similarities; apart from anything else, states now in existence have been influenced in their formation by the sacred and secular images of David and Solomon, Athens and Sparta, Augustus and Constantine. But there are differences too, so that we distort or deny *our* state and its possibilities if we force them into the straitjacket of ancient examples. The modern state is modern. Our state system is, in large part, a post-medieval European development. The novelty came into view in the Treaty of Westphalia of 1648, in which the nations decided the basic shape and principles of the modern European inter-state system amongst themselves, ignoring Pope Innocent X's fulminations against a treaty 'null and void, accursed and without any influence or result for the past, the present, or the future'.[2] And in other respects, the state, as we know it, has developed even more recently. It is arguable that dominating features of the state today have appeared in the last one hundred years with Bismarck as its symbol. War, cultural engineering and welfare have enlarged the state's activities, and made it inescapable for all of us for good or

---

1. Cf. Karl Barth, *Evangelical Theology: An Introduction* (London, 1963); G. K. Chesterton, *The Man Who was Thursday*.

2. G. R. Cragg, *The Church and the Age of Reason (1648-1789)* (Harmondsworth, 1960), pp. 9f. Cf. M. Donelan (ed.), *The Reason of States* (London, 1978), chap. 1.

ill.[3] Down to the time of Erasmus it was no hardship to be a wandering scholar. Indeed, down to 1914, one could travel through Europe without a passport. But who would choose to be stateless today? The omnipresence of the modern state puts it on the agenda for Christian social ethics in a way that may not have been the case in the past. It would be wrong to suggest that no theological attention has been given to the modern state, but in England, at least, it has not been very serious, coherent or effective in enabling Christians to have a common mind and a message that makes saving sense of the state. We oscillate in an unprincipled way between support for and denigration of the modern state. Sometimes we interpret the modern state as though it stands in the tradition of Egypt under Joseph's direction as interpreted favourably in *Joseph and his Amazing Technicoloured Dream Coat* —

> Seven years of famine followed —
> Egypt didn't mind a bit:
> the first recorded rationing in history was a hit.

In another mood, to explain the same characteristics of the state, we descry the dragon of Rev. 13 causing all to have the mark upon their foreheads as the condition of sharing in buying and selling. We must get beyond this selective, magpie, dilettante use of the Bible.

Romans 13

It will, of course, be said that I am making the problem too difficult. The Bible, you may say, does speak plainly, theologically and ethically, about the state in one or two places, in ways which prevent oscillation under pressure of circumstances between positive and negative views of the state. Moreover, what the Bible says transcends differences between the state of biblical times and the state today. Romans 13:1-7 is the best example, if not almost the only one to be found in the New Testament. It is at least the only one I have space to discuss here. And it should be noted that I am discussing it from a limited point of view: I am asking

3. E. P. Hennock, *Fit and Proper Persons* (London, 1973), especially pp. 61ff., 154ff., 295ff.

whether it speaks theologically — in a way we can make our own — of the state as we have it and are likely to have it nowadays. The brief answer is 'No'. There is a great deal in this text that we can accept without difficulty, not least its assurance that God is over all.[4] But I at least do not find· it easy to make sense of the particular way in which it understands God to be over all things and of some of the consequences it draws. In particular, verse 3, 'For rulers are not a terror to good conduct, but to bad', does not describe any state we know or might make. Our own country is no exception. We can be thankful that we do not for the most part have government by terror and atrocity. But it cannot be claimed that we have government which puts no obstacles or disincentives in the way of doing good. Our tax and social security systems, for example, do not uniformly encourage goodness, a sense of fairness, enthusiasm for hard work and enterprise, the values of the family. The larger the state gets the more important are its ambiguous effects on people's motivation and values.

We have all heard it said that Socialism stifles initiative — and Toryism erodes compassion. Now, it may be replied that the state, the cabinet and the civil service — the real government — are always better than the rhetoric of the competing parties suggests. In fact it is often argued that parties pathologically distort the real issues, dividing and polarising unnecessarily and thwarting good government.[5] But that is merely to say that, blinded by fear and ambition in the political battle, the parties misconstrue the specific failings of government, not that there is a state (above parties) without fault. Government on this view is still a disincentive to good works, but the fault is now seen to lie with the party system. However illuminating that may be as analysis of our political problems, it does not affect the issue — for in the terms of Romans 13 the party system should be counted as *part* of the powers that be in our country. They are disincentives to virtue — to fellowship and efficiency — *because* of the party system, without which our state would not be itself.

Moreover, even if it were true that our state in fact did good, we must reckon with the fact that the political processes by which it is worked are democratic. That not merely

4. Cf. E. Käsemann, 'Principles of the Interpretation of Romans 13' in *New Testament Questions of Today* (London, 1969), pp. 196-216; *An die Römer* (Tübingen, 1974), pp. 338-339.
5. S. E. Finer (ed.), *Adversary Politics and Electoral Reform* (London, 1975).

stands in some tension with Paul's view of the divine ordina-
tion of the state and the consequent duty of submission. Less
easy to handle is the assumption institutionalized in our kind
of democracy, that governments are fallible, likely to misuse
and be corrupted by the power they have. That basic assumption is not compatible with Romans 13:3. So our politics
which institutionalize opposition have as part of their
rhetoric the continual accusing of government as being a terror to good works — and this is more than rhetoric. The
history of the development of our democratic, parliamentary
state is also the history of a people's experience of the
political unworkability of Romans 13 and of their attempts to
cope with its consequences.

So then Romans 13 does not outline a theology of the state
which we can take over. There are common ways of using the
passage which do not do the text the credit of taking it
seriously. Many Evangelicals may find the state as we know it
'as *by and large* concerned for the good' — but there is no
qualifying 'by and large' in Paul's words. Some say 'Paul
knew that no state was like his description'[6] but why then did
he bother to write what turned out to be a momentously influential text which many have taken to endorse states like
Nero's and Hitler's, taking verse 1 so concretely as to
evacuate verse 3 of any force? Or was Paul simply saying
government as compared to anarchic chaos is a good thing?
That is an agreeable sentiment which endorses our positive interest in the state in principle, but it does not begin to do the
theology of the state for us, or tell us how it should be done.

States in the Bible

If the Bible does not give us a theology of the state directly in
a text like Romans 13:1ff., does it offer one indirectly, if one
reads between the lines? When its whole story is read does it
open up some perspectives within which the state is illumi-
nated theologically? Perhaps it does: for the state appears
repeatedly in its story of the saving works of God in the
history of his people. On closer consideration, however, the
state seems to be no more than part of the earthly *context* of
the story of the people of God. Sometimes they are in conflict
with the state, sometimes they benefit from it. In David and
Solomon and their successors, God's way with his people

6. These suggestions came from some of the Conference discussion groups as a
response to this paper.

takes stately form, but that arrangement did not last. The
prophets re-opened the distinction between God's way with
his people and the state, accepting the disasters of political
history as the judgement of God. Out of this history, the
kingdom of David is left to the New Testament as a symbol
for the kingdom of God, a kingdom which Jesus is reported
to have said is not of this world (Jn. 18:36), and was not
going to be restored to Israel in that future which is our
responsibility (Acts 1:6,7). The state is the stage setting for
part of the play, not it seems, one of the *dramatis personae*,
and when the story moves on, so the scene is changed and the
state disappears from view. Take as an example the story of
Joseph in Egypt. Egypt is the nearest the biblical world gets
to our kind of centralized state, and Joseph becomes the ruler
of it. It might look as though this story would provide a
model of our kind of state under God's statesman, and that a
positive theology of the state might be drawn from it. But the
interest of the story focuses narrowly on 'Jacob and Sons'
and God's dealings with them. That is why the narrative has
no sensitivity about Joseph's inhumanity when he exploited
the famine to buy up all the people's land and flocks, thus
reducing them to slavery (Gen. 47:13ff.). Anyone interested in
the state in itself might notice that such an oppressive extension of state power, such hard bargaining, does not fit morally with the giving and interpreting of Pharoah's dreams
which were intended to enable Egypt to be prepared for
famine and so to be brought through it. Moreover, it is the
kind of conduct law and prophets denounced. In short, there
is no coherent theory of the state in this story which can be
affirmed by any one who has a biblical view of God or man.
But Genesis is untroubled. It is interested in Joseph, not the
state, so it records the process as another sign that God was
with Joseph and he was (in Tyndale's words) a lucky fellow.
Of course, it still happens that politicians use the state as
though it existed to further their personal career, their family
fortunes or the concerns of the powerful but we do not want
to take such statemanship as a theological model. It offends
both Christian and secular moral sense to approve what may
admittedly have to be endured.

I am aware that this is a one-sided abbreviated summary of
the Bible's presentation of the state. But it is one side. It must
be reckoned with carefully if we want a biblical theology of
the state rather than an eclectic exploitation of some of the
Bible's sayings and stories (which will be vulnerable to con-

tradiction derived from other sayings and stories). It appears
that when the Bible tells stories which involve the state, it is
not concerned with the state and it need not surprise us if
little or no coherent theology of the state with ethical grip is
to be seen in them.

The formation of the new international people, the church,
in the New Testament seems to strengthen the barrier between the way of God's people in this world and the state.
The lack of interest in the state now becomes more of a conscious non-negotiable theological principle. At least, so it has
often been interpreted. The church is made up of the regener-
ate to whom more is possible ethically than to the citizens and
rulers of the state in general. The promise of the Gospel and
its way is true and real within the church, within the personal
and small community spheres where spiritual spontaneity
operates and everything may be done in conscious faith. The
gospel belongs to believers, and so its interpretation of the
nature of human existence, its ethics and its promise are
available in church, but not in the state, for the state does
not, and cannot, believe the gospel. A great gulf seems fixed
between what the church knows is true and demanding and
effective for itself, and what is possible for the world.

The New Testament speaks in a theological idiom to which
the distinction between church and non-church seems essential. It is a high dividing wall which stands in the way of the
development of a theology of the state. The wall is broken
through in conversion — but conversion is individual and
personal. We, after the end of Christendom, no longer hope
for the conversion of the state; most of us would not believe it
was real conversion if it seemed to happen. The wall may
somehow be broken at the end of time, when the kings of the
earth will bring their glory and honour into the heavenly
Jerusalem (Rev. 22:24). But, of course, a theology of the
state must talk about what exists now, before that has come
to pass. What meaning (if any) have all those things, including the state, which fill up the times before the end? Certainly when reading Revelation one is tempted to say that the
meaning of the state is the wrath of God and the endurance
of the saints. That is, simply, there is a sharp distinction
between state and gospel, state and church.

Viewing the State from the Gospel

The Bible, then, does not give us a ready-made theology of

the state and even does a good deal to discourage the quest for one. Should we not accept the verdict of the Bible? Yet if we give up the quest we encounter a problem which Howard Marshall tackled in his paper in relation to demonology. Whatever reasons we as biblical Christians may have for not having a positive or theological view of the state, few if any of us practise accordingly. We do not live in an apocalyptic state nor do we want to. We are involved with and dependent on the state. Practically we have a positive view of it. Many of us serve the state or are paid more or less directly by it, without objecting, even with enthusiasm. The good order of the state enables us in some measure to be and do good. So we have good reason for not wishing its breakdown. The reading of the New Testament which I have been reporting would impel us into a standing inconsistency with ourselves. We need a more positive theology of the state to make honest men and women of ourselves. We do not really believe in the state as wrath of God. It gets nearer to what most of us believe to see the state as part of what may take place here and now, thanks to the creative forgiving and the mysterious patience of God. And that theme we should explore theologically. It turns out, so I believe, against first appearances, to be what the heart of the gospel commits us to.

There are two reasons why our first ways of looking at the biblical history and the New Testament yielded no adequate theology of the state. First, we were merely doing concordance work (looking up 'state' and trying to collate into a coherent picture all the references to it in the Bible) and not theological work, which is the attempt to think of, from and for God, Father, Son and Holy Spirit. Secondly, we noted the division the gospel has produced between church and non-church, as though we were historical observers studying only on the church side or even having some viewpoint above the world. Thus we saw that the historical, communal, institutional *outcome* of Christ is division between those believingly conscious of the gospel and those not. There is another way of reading the gospel, from the inside. We may identify with and participate in the *process*, which is the gospel, living in its spirit, which grieves over the division, as Christ wept over Jerusalem (Lk. 19:41), reaches out beyond it in love and hope and does not accept the division as irremediably fixed. From this viewpoint what determines a Christian theology of the state is not the inescapable distinction of church and state, but the way of God in Christ, the gospel, which we believe by living in and by it.

I need not remind you that God's way in Jesus is the way of
the justification of the ungodly. While we were yet sinners
Christ died for us — that is the way of God's love for the
world. God's love was not, and so is not, reserved for those
who love him, or merit it. God's love is movingly active
before we turn to him: 'while we were yet sinners' (Rom.
5:6ff.). At this point, the distinction between church and
non-church no longer determines us (2 Cor. 5:14ff.). The
church exists and stands only because there is a God who
justifies the ungodly, a God who does not wait for their per-
mission to enact his love for them. The church believes in him
and that is why it is happy to be the church. By believing that,
however, its mere existence must become a sign of hope for
the world. For the world now may see itself in the church —
and learns that the world is not to be determined by its own
sin — there is a God who is sovereign and who forgives; that
is, when the chips are down, he is not determined in what he
does to his creatures by what they do to him.

The church believes this good news, this incredible exciting
news. That is what makes it church. But given the content of
the message, with the process and passion of God which the
message discloses, it cannot believe it for itself unless it
believes it for others. Evangelicalism has insisted that each
must accept Christ for himself; but that breeds an individualism which is not evangelical, true to gospel. The gospel says:
Each must accept that Christ died for the other man, for
other people, for all. 'Because he died for all', one can say,
'even I have some hope, some right to think he died for me
because I am one of that "all".' We are forgiven — so we
forgive. And the forgiveness comes out of that free recreative
initiative of God which is what we put our trust in. To the
exercise of forgiveness we are called. We are reconciled —
because he who knew no sin did not hold fast to his purity but
was made sin for us, that we might be made the righteousness
of God in him. And what is that righteousness? It is to be
discovered as we take up the ministry of reconciliation, in our
turn and in the same love that God in Christ showed.

God's becoming man in the incarnation is his moving to
the other — man — showing himself to be for the other. This
is the love which God is; as creator, judge and redeemer, he is
essentially for the other. Jesus is the man for others. He is a
social being and socially creative. In his being and action he
includes others. He is not simply individual.

In his ministry, he attacked the leaders because they did not
exist for others and did not bring them into community as
their office required. He himself gathered and shepherded the
lost sheep of the house of Israel, neglected by the official
shepherds. When his disciples told him to send the crowds
away to get food he said, '*You* give them something to eat'.
The gospel to the elder brother is not an unnecessary invita-
tion to return to the home he never left, but to rejoice at the
return of the other, the prodigal sinner. The life of Jesus is
the sign of the gospel in this repeated variegated turning to
the other, by which he included tax-collectors and sinners in
fellowship. Only those were left out who refused to see that
the inclusion of sinners, the ultimate others, is the good
news.[7] Jesus did not actually include everybody, but the
movement of his mission was this unresting seeking for the
lost. The universality is implicit; incomplete but inescapable.
Our following in the way of Jesus is always drawn on by the
same universal horizons.

Universally for Others

Now in relation to the gospel both church and state stand
under the same call (or the same condemnation when they
disobey). They are not universal in their practice or intention.
They are *called* to universality but they do not fulfil it. But
while we should criticize, we should be slow to condemn. For
the logic and spirit of the gospel is not to dismiss the sinner
from service and hope, but to forgive him by enabling him to
begin again and serve fruitfully. In the spirit of the gospel the
same goes for people gathered and ordered in institutions,
like church and state. They are imperfect, inadequate. They
fall short of their calling. Churches and states hover between
exclusive tribalism and tentative reaching out towards the
fullness of God's family in heaven and earth.[8] We who know
the gospel should pray for and foster that partial but real
reaching out to others which is institutionalized in church and
state, rather than write them off when they fall short.

Mrs. Thatcher once contrasted the Good Samaritan and
the welfare state. She would put more faith in spontaneous
unorganized neighbourliness than bureaucratic provision. I

7. Cf. Haddon Willmer (ed.), *Christian Faith and Political Hopes* (London,
1979), pp. 127ff.
8. D.E. Jenkins, *The Contradiction of Christianity* (London, 1976), chap. 1.

wonder what the Good Samaritan would say about it. I fancy
that he would have said that uncoerced neighbourliness is
part of the joy of being human in God's image and fellowship. But he might say that it would also have been good to
have a state which encouraged priests and levites to be more
neighbourly, that discouraged the unneighbourliness of
thieves, and that (since the Good Samaritan would not be on
the road every day, though people have accidents there every
day) it would be good to set aside someone to be on permanent watch. The feeding of the five thousand roots the work
of Tear Fund in the gospel although Tear Fund's operations
have more similarities with a state's methods than the miracle
of Jesus. In the same way, the state as systematic and extended love of neighbours is a form of the Good Samaritan.
In the state, the Good Samaritan may be given a longer reach
— the *sign* of God's love given something more of that
abiding presence, that ever watchfulness, that faithfulness
which are characteristic of God in his heavenly fullness. And
the Good Samaritan is the man on God's side, the man who
responds to and shares in the love of God by practising it.[9]

The basic movement — towards others, for others, to
affirm, uphold and improve their being in fellowship together
— which occurs savingly in Jesus Christ and in God's election
of his old and new peoples is also fundamentally but not un-
ambiguously characteristic of the state. Out of faithfulness to
the gospel, a theology of the state will make much of this
possibility; it is no more than posssibility. When we decline to
interpret the state theologically in these hopeful and demanding Christocentric terms, theology practically denies the
gospel by failing to be 'for others', having the kind of out-
reach with wide horizons that is revealed in Jesus Christ. Do
we have a gospel 'for others' as individuals, but not for
others as they are bonded together in the forms and activities
of the state?

In David Cook's terms, I am asking for the development of
a participant existentialist theology of the state, not an
observer theology. The state is a possibility we as people
redeemed to humanity in Christ are called to seek to realize,
in so far as it may be an instrument for fulfilling our human
calling to love our neighbour effectively. The state is not
given ready-made. It is continually made or not made by
people so that they may be together by being for one another.

9. This was written before I had seen R. Sider, *Rich Christians in an Age of
Hunger* (London, 1978), pp. 177ff.

We all share in realizing or blocking the possibility, willingly or unwillingly. The state that relies democratically on its citizens is likely, so Bernard Crick argues, to be more effective as a state as well as more open than a coercive undemocratic one.[10] But there is no state that can exist without getting its members somehow to contribute to its making.

If the state is a human task, a human calling, and that human calling is defined in Jesus Christ, Christians must seek to participate in all states, even if the only participation allowed by the powers that be is to pay taxes, to obey the good laws and suffer for resisting the bad and to pray. Prayer can hardly be stopped, but we are reminded of the subversive significance of political prayer by the story of Daniel. To pray for the state is also to confess its sins and lament its short-comings, and to open it before God, if there be no other forum, to the disturbing vocation of being human. The Christian certainly wants fuller participation, a more open and neighbourly life than such a state is likely to foster. Neighbourly love cannot be encouraged very much by a state that does not trust and enable its members to work for each other. But in all states, following the way of Christ points in that direction and will exploit every opportunity of moving along that way.

Critical and Supportive

It is clear that this approach yields a positive affirmation of the state as a calling, as human possibility; it is supportive. But it is also critical; it gives us a plain yet inexhaustible criterion for judging the state. As we know too well, the state as organized people, or public person 'for others', is in practice more often empty promise than successful performance. The state — or those who possess its commanding heights — often exploits its profession of being for others and serving human values in order to maintain its grip on gullible people whom it uses and even destroys. Then the state denies its promise which is in harmony with God's way. Because the state or man in the state has a *real* possibility of being for others, its not being for others is so painful a disappointment, so grave a guilt and so unnecessary a lost opportunity.

10. Bernard Crick, *The Reform of Parliament* (2nd edn., London, 1970), p. 18.

But it will be said, the theologian ought to know before-
hand that the failure is inevitable, for the state and man in the
state are both fallen. There has been a good deal of talk about
the fall in this conference, and it seems to me we have a lot
more work to do on its significance for social ethics.
I would like to make two comments. First, according to the
doctrine, nothing human is unfallen. Therefore it may not be
used selectively to explain the difference between relatively
successful and unsuccessful human enterprises as though only
the latter are fallen. The relatively good is as much fallen as
the relatively bad. In our practical concern for the state, we
do not expect unfallen perfection; we are concerned for pre-
ferring and fostering the relatively good as much as possible.
Remember Paul's qualifications in Rom. 12:18, '*If possible,
so far as it depends on you,* live peaceably with all'. Even
though we are all fallen, practising such relative distinctions is
possible and worthwhile. Secondly, it follows that Christians
are not to interpret the fall as though it dooms to hopeless-
ness every human endeavour. For Christians do not *believe in*
the fall. They believe in God the Redeemer and they think
with him in and about the world and themselves. God's preservation of the murderer Cain, a kind of shadow of redemption, is a sign that from the beginning God did not let fallenness and evil have a free course. The coupling of the execu-
tion of judgement and the restraint of destructive revenge is
part of the essence of the state (Gen. 4:9-15).

Christians approach the state hopefully, because they think
in terms of the 'for-other' reality of the gospel. Whether they
expect little or much from the state, they ought to find it interesting that in the state (as in other human organizations of
which it is an example), both the supportive and the critical
are present in a variety of its institutions and processes.

On the supportive side, there can be no state without institutions which create power out of the energies of a crowd
of people, power with intelligible and usable forms. To make
laws and take decisions about what the community will be
and do requires particular kinds of power, which must be
fashioned out of available resources, above all, out of people
who in the state become citizens. But the state is not only the
making and making available of power; it also must include
the direction of power, through institutions and processes of
criticism, checking and balancing. To exist, states need both
'body' and 'will' and on the critical side, 'intelligence' and
'conscience'. The police are a stark example here. A people

without police are not a secure or efficient community. So police power must be created by and for community. But once made, police power must be controlled or it will work against community. This example of course points us to urgent practical tasks in our own country as elsewhere. If the state is both the making and the criticism of communal power, for the fulfilment of the human vocation in the way of Christ, we can expect that the Christian affirmation and criticism of the state can be played out within the political process, not just by commenting on it from outside. As citizens and politicians we may live the Christian life within the processes of the state, and we may work with other men, who are not Christians, but whose thinking and action is shaped by their participation in the human task of the state, so that it takes on in some measure the 'for-other' character of God's way.

Conflict and Coercion

There has been no room in this paper for descriptions of the modern state and states, but I hope it may be evident that some of the essential elements of the state that the reader cannot help but be acquainted with are being spoken of, albeit with an abstractness that derives more from brevity than theology. It is well to emphasize that the state is not unitary or simple, however much the way we speak about it may give that impression. It is complex and conflictual. The social, industrial, and ethnic conflicts of peoples and traditions take on stately form (e.g. devolution and the 'United Kingdom'). Further, because the state has a multiplicity of tasks and purposes, in response to various real or felt needs, it develops manifold institutions so that conflict gets institutionalized in its framework and policies. There is a tension between the Treasury and spending departments, or between education and industry (as the Green Paper on Education, 1978, showed). The mere existence of the state as coercive (however gentle and just it may be) provokes conflict with a humanity properly dreaming of freedom and so feeling oppressed.[11] The state is one form of human reckoning with the coercive limits of created existence. It has an uncertain relation with finitude; it embodies and enacts a general recognition of

11. Barrington Moore, Jr., *Reflections on the Causes of Human Misery and upon Certain Proposals to Eliminate them* (London, 1970), pp. 32, 47.

finitude but at the same time, it is not bound to accept any one particular finite order as necessary.[12] So, for example, we may agree there ought to be a wages policy because there is, at any point in time, only a finite cake to share, but 'we' leave ourselves free to refuse a policy which would bear hardly on our group, because 'we' count ourselves a special case. If all groups decline to accept at least some share of the burden of finitude, the state as a recognition of the general fact of finitude becomes unjust or unworkable or both. To this insecurity in principle of the state must be added its ambiguity. Sometimes it uses its coercive powers to organize people to defy the coercive limits of their situation (and so a nation is made to fight to the death or the U.S.A. wastes resources to put the first man on the moon). Or we may use coercive powers to enable us to perceive more accurately what are the limits of human being and how we may live harmoniously and hopefully with and within them. Both the police and the present-day ecological and environmental debates are relevant examples here. They both illustrate that it is not enough to define the state as conflictual. The state exists only where there is some measure of social and more than momentary *resolution* of the conflicts which are inherent in man's social existence and action. The state has value precisely because running conflict and unresolved clashes of interest are not to be lived with. However conflictual its components the state cannot be described simply in terms of them.

Forgiveness and Futility

Even when power-making and power-criticizing functions are present, states may still fail for lack of adequate resolution of the conflicts between these aspects. They may even not get that far, they may not be able to build power adequate to the situation they are in; or they may fail in self-criticism, either by complacency or by judging themselves by inadequate criteria. The state is always in some measure a failure — like most human enterprises — sometimes a total failure. Whether it knows it or not, the state survives failure by something akin to that forgiveness of God which is his mercy over all his works. There is a dark night of institutions, as David Jenkins has called it. The state lives through a cross and finds renewal like life from the dead in the vocation to

12. Cf. Arthur Koestler, *Arrow in the Blue* (Danube edition, Hutchinson, London, 1969), pp. 348-349.

being human together. There might here be the call for a
special Christian ministry to the state. For the state desperately seeks permanence in a world where everything passes away,
and all language becomes self-justificatory in politics where it
is made so costly to admit mistakes. The pride of the state
which appears essential to its being is a destructive guilt,
through which it denies and loses its humanity, pretending it
is as God. It is not: a state lives, like everything human, by
the patience and forgiveness of God.

The church witnesses to forgiveness, not least by sharing in
the ministry of forgiveness. When the state falters or fails, we
experience what Paul calls *futility* in Romans 8:20. In a creation that promises so much, the good seems so long in coming, or is thwarted before it bears fruit. Politics is littered
with the debris of unfinished enterprises, lost opportunities,
seemingly insoluble problems like N. Ireland and unbearable
pains like the Holocaust and the long-drawn-out hunger of
millions to which no end is as yet in sight. No wonder people
become apathetic about the state especially as an instrument
for fulfilling the human vocation. At this low point it is not
ethics we need so much as theology, or better a gospel, faith
and spirituality, as in Romans 8, that hopes and shares hope
for salvation even in and for this world.

I think we have sometimes talked in this conference as
though if only we were to get our social ethics right, we
should be able to do the right thing and escape the confusions
and mistakes of politics as we know them. That is only half
the story and on its own it is untrue. It may indeed be
altogether untrue.

For life, and politics, continually requires us to make decisions with inadequate knowledge or wisdom or goodwill — to
act out of weakness — and so to blunder on into futility.
Ethics will not save us from that at every point. What we need
is to be ready and able to live through the mistakes we make.
The kind of permanence the state may rightly seek to have is
not unbroken, simple continuance but repeated renewal,
within and against futility. Let us, in and for the state and so
effectively for man, trust and look to God who raises the
dead, and not rely on even the best ethics with its delusory
perfectionist promise. We should affirm the state supportive-
ly and critically, as a human enterprise, because in itself, even
in its futility, it is also a standing resistance to despair in the
midst of futility. We should also criticize and resist the state
when it allies itself with the denial of futility, when it grasps

heaven, Babel-like, or accepts inhumanity with resignation, or when it is the agent of all that makes futility seem the real end of this world.

Reading List

J. H. Yoder, *The Christian Witness to the State* (Newton, Kansas, 1964).

U. Simon, *A Theology of Auschwitz* (London, 1978).

E.W. Lefever (ed.), *Ethics and World Politics: Four Perspectives* (Baltimore, 1972).

Karl Barth, *Against the Stream* (London, 1954).

D. A. Lane (ed.), *Liberation Theology — an Irish Dialogue* (Dublin, 1977).

Industrial Mission Association, *Theology and Politics* (Manchester, 1978).

H. Willmer (ed.), *Christian Faith and Political Hopes* (London, 1979).

Questions for Discussion

1   How recent a development is the state as we know it today, and what future has it got? How should such considerations affect the development of a theology of the state?

2   Does the Bible give us a ready-made theology of the state, or at least a do-it-yourself kit with clear instructions?
If yes: what is it?
If no: what is the next move?

3   What does the unity of God mean if we cannot rely on God to be the same God for all men, or the same in both church and state? If he is the same, what is the real difference between church and state?

4   Is Jesus Christ the 'one word of God' (Barmen Declaration) or is the theology of the state to be developed on some other basis?

5   What promise of an adequate theological ethic of the
     state is there in the style of argument revolving round the
     calling of the citizen, as used in the Koinonia Declara-
     tion, e.g. para. 2:

     The Bible gives us guidelines as to what the duties of the
     citizen as well as civil government are. Accordingly we believe
     that it is the duty of the civil government to protect everybody
     within its territory, and further that each man has the right to
     such protection, in order to enable him to do good, that is, to
     fulfil his calling (without obstruction by anyone whatsoever)
     towards God and therefore also towards his neighbour as his
     fellow citizen and fellow human being, in all human relation-
     ships. This means *inter alia* that:

     i. the citizen as a human being has the divinely ordained right
        and duty of displaying charity, that is, *inter alia,* in being
        merciful, practising community, promoting justice and
        mutual admonition, towards all people, irrespective of who
        they are, and especially to the weak and underprivileged;

     ii. no responsible Christian can properly exercise his calling and
         duties with regard to a political society unless (a) he is able to
         obtain sufficient information, having a bearing on his calling
         and/or duties in the State; (b) he is able to freely express his
         responsible opinion and his right to be heard is acknow-
         ledged.

6   What theological bases are there for Christian loyalty to
     the *imperfect* state, or must we choose between com-
     promises that go against conscience and a principled
     anarchist opposition to the state?

Chapter Five
The Challenge of Marxism
David Lyon

CHAPTER FIVE
The Challenge of Marxism*

IT IS THE CLARION CALL OF LATIN AMERICAN CHRISTIANS
which poses the challenge of Marxism most acutely: '. . .
revolutionary action aimed at changing the basic economic,
political, social, and cultural structures and conditions of life
is imperative today in the world'.[1] Thus speaks the Argentine
José Míguez Bonino. To most western Christians, who have
for over a century uncritically accepted the *status quo* of
capitalist development as generally beneficent to the human
race, it comes as a sudden shock.

Biblical Christians have difficulties in responding to the
challenge of Marxism, mainly because the challenge is so
complex. Questions are raised about the nature of Marxism
itself, and its twentieth-century historical record. The issue of
Christian witness in different social and cultural contexts,
and the importance attached to those contexts, is also high-
lighted. Above all, perhaps, the nature of Christian commitment (with the spectre of social gospels ever peering over
one's shoulder) comes in for radical scrutiny.

The aim of this paper is fourfold. First we shall examine
the resurgence of Marxism in Britain in the 1970s, especially
in higher education and in the practical politics of unionism.
Secondly, we shall look briefly at Marx's Marxism and the
Marxism of his subsequent interpreters. What are Marxism's

*See note at end of chapter (p. 128).
1. José Míguez Bonino, *Christians and Marxists* (London, 1976), p. 8.

distinguishing features, and what are the main bones of contention? Thirdly, we shall ask why biblical people have had such an aversion to Marxism and what factors are now causing us to rethink that position. Lastly, we shall attempt to outline an alternative to Marxism which is both compatible with biblical faith, and yet offers a response to the insistent challenge of Marxist commitment.

Why Marxism?

The perennial fascination of Marxism is both intellectual and moral. Marxism is a world-view of compelling force and relevance, as much today as a century ago. George Bernard Shaw admitted that Marx had touched in him and others a chord of hatred 'for the middle-class institutions that had starved, thwarted, misled, and corrupted them spiritually from their cradles'.[2] Here is the moral critique: things are not as they should be, nor even what we have been led to believe they are. But how do we know? Marx's answer was, by study. As Nicholas Berdyaev wrote: 'Marx was intellectual; he ascribed immense importance to theory, philosophy, science; he did not believe in the type of politics which is based on the emotions; he ascribed enormous importance to the development of thought and organization.'[3]

Marxism is radical and comprehensive. It attempts to account for reality as such, never limiting itself to a small component specialism. Thus its religious pretensions are unmasked. Moreover, it simultaneously evokes moral indignation and open-minded analysis, touching the world at highly sensitive points. Lastly, it integrates into one scheme disciplined thought and practical action. Marx disdained both the ivory tower myopia of utopian socialism and the mindless anarchic rebellion of a Bakunin. In Marx's praxis 'the philosophers have only interpreted the world in various ways; the point is to change it'.[4]

Marx's intellectual critique has always appealed in the British context. Ever since evangelical defector H. M. Hyndman discovered a new gospel in Marx and founded the Social Democratic Federation, a strand of highly educated Marx-followers has influenced left-wing opinion. Literate and per-

2. N. and J. MacKenzie, *The First Fabians* (London, 1977), p. 40.
3. Nicholas Berdyaev, *The Origins of Russian Communism* (London, 1937), p. 67.
4. Marx, 'Theses on Feuerbach' (1844), *KMSW*, p. 158.

suasive academics — such as Ralph Miliband in political science and E. P. Thompson in history — are now instructing a new generation of university students in a sophisticated mode of Marxist analysis.

Working class groups are also affected by Marxism, but this has never amounted to overwhelming mass support. The Socialist Workers' Party is forever bemoaning the decline of broad class-consciousness which has in recent years been replaced by shop-floor-level do-it-yourself reformism. Their complaint is that short-term gains tend to eclipse revolutionary hopes, and that all governments tend to base their industrial relations policies on this fact. Nevertheless, the SWP have not yet tired of echoing Marx's battle-cry: 'the emancipation of the working class must be the work of the working class itself'.[5]

It is the *interaction* between theory and practice which gives Marxism continued mileage in the late twentieth century. The Socialist Workers' Party have to educate their members with analyses of current British capitalism, to enable them to see the context of their struggles. And those struggles are no longer confined to the shop-floor. Oppression has now been discovered at the kitchen sink and in the social services department. Social theory and analysis beget the discovery of public ills; the discovery of social ills begets social theory.

The notorious 'Gould Report' on Marxist penetration in higher education, published in 1977,[6] drew attention to what most people knew anyway, that Marx is alive and well in the British university. Despite the hopeful declaration of the 'end of ideology' by certain social thinkers at the end of the 1950s, academic interest in Marx has increasingly flourished. Marxism is probably at its strongest in seminar-rooms and student unions. 'Bourgeois' publishers such as Macmillan and Penguin churn out best-selling academic Marxisms of all shades. The 'what-Marx-really-meant' debate has never been so fierce.

Social Sciences

Post-war reconstruction spawned the social sciences in the

5. Marx, circular letter to Bebel *et al.*, quoted in *International Socialism* 100 (1977), p. 3.

6. J. Gould (ed.)., *The Attack on Higher Education: Marxist and Radical Penetration* (London, 1977).

late 50s and 60s, and it is this new form of social understanding and criticism which has exposed the seamier aspects of modern 'civilization', giving grist to the Marxist mill. The we've-never-had-it-so-good syndrome of the 50s gave way in the late 60s to the realization that the definition of 'good' left much unsaid. 'Good for whom?' is the question which still hangs over the statistics of inequality and the citadels of industrial alienation.

The same question is urgently raised over the so-called Welfare State. Marxists argue, with some justification, that the welfare apparatus really serves to maintain the age-old class-distinctions and divisions of British society, and ensures that certain interest groups perpetuate their hegemony. This had given rise to a new brand of (partly) Marx-inspired thinking in social policy, with accompanying practice in radical social work and community work.

The most insidious aspect of the Welfare State, according to some, is its pervasive repressive ideology. Crucial to this, it is said, is the Protestant work ethic, and a belief in the uniqueness of family life. But the weakening of moral constraints, plus the existentialist thrust to do one's own thing, radically challenges this. In particular, there is a new women's consciousness. Beveridge may have thought that the family is sacrosanct, but this is often now regarded as mere capitalist eyewash. The Welfare State not only bolsters capitalism by ameliorating the worst conditions it produces, thus defusing discontent, it also maintains the system by defining people's life-roles for them.

Women are not the only ones to have given a fillip to Marxist analysis in the 1970s; the whole gamut of sexual politics has injected new meanings into words like 'exploitation' and 'oppression'. Gay Liberation sees itself as a signpost to new relationships normally denied under capitalist rule (although not all Marxists would recognize the connection between the gay cause and theirs).

All this shows that it is very difficult to pin down the reasons for Marxism's current vogue: they are manifold. There is the undeniable influence of world affairs, especially the romantic attraction of liberation movements in the Third World, often with a strong Marxist flavour. Repudiating the legacy of colonialism and imperialism in such countries apparently necessitates a swing to the opposite extreme by way of compensation. And as China's achievement becomes more public to western eyes, the usual selective amnesia sets in as health, welfare, and distributive equality are seen as the only products of Maoism.

Industrial relations, fraught with strife which is often encouraged by both 'sides', may legitimately be viewed as the arena of class-struggles. Groups on the left glory in the miners' strikes which 'brought down the Heath government' in the early 70s, and look forward to further major confrontations which will eventually bring down capitalism itself. That the actions of both Conservative (Industrial Relations Act) and Labour (Social Contract) parties can be interpreted as obstructive to significant social change gives fuel to the left-wing commentators and activists.

An opportunity to work out an intellectual Marxist critique of contemporary society is afforded by the growth of the social sciences and their application in fields such as social policy and town planning. It began with the desire to apply 'science' to human social welfare, but in an age when the 'neutrality' of science was still largely unquestioned. Things are different now.

Lastly, it must be said that the advanced industrial society of capitalistic Britain can afford to allow minority opinions to flourish, without fear of revolution. The holders and controllers of resources in Britain are in a strong enough position to allow such steam to be let off. The media, for example, so powerfully and faithfully reflect the *status quo* that deviant opinion is unlikely to gain a foothold, especially in places where that foothold might count.

Which Marxism?

Marx himself remained to the end of his days a revolutionary socialist. Others, while believing in the desirability of socialism, have opted for other routes to that goal. This is why many whose social eyes have been opened by Marx, would not necessarily associate themselves with his name. They wish to avoid the violent, revolutionary connotations of Marxism.

The question of 'which Marxism?' is not abstractly academic: it connects vitally with political and ethical reality. Human lives and community destinies are involved, so that the debate over 'which Marxism?' has always been intense, and sometimes bitterly fought. The fact that intolerable human misery has forced the question onto the Christian agenda in recent years makes it more than an academic question for us too.

In the British context, various paths to socialism (not Marxism) were mooted in the nineteenth century. First, there were attempts like Robert Owen's, at the New Lanark Mills, to set up working alternatives to capitalism. Such utopian communities were intended to demonstrate the non-inevitability of exploitation and oppression in industrial development. Co-operation was put forward as a manifestly achievable alternative to competition.[7]

Secondly, there was an attitude which may be represented by John Stuart Mill.[8] Towards the end of his life, he was increasingly drawn towards socialism as a means of ensuring a better quality of life for all. His approach was an appeal to the powerful on the grounds of reason and justice, assuming, of course, that they would listen.

Britain has never boasted a popular representative leader of the third path: revolution. Marx himself, an astute observer of the British scene, more than once admitted the possibility of a peaceful transition to socialism in Britain.[9] But in other European countries there were socialists who believed in a mass rising of the exploited, or a conspiracy of a revolutionary party.

The fourth path, that of the democratic and parliamentary ascendancy of a socialist party, became a viable possibility too late in the nineteenth century for Marx to comment on it at length. But movements like Hyndman's SDF and Keir Hardie's Independent Labour Party were to lay the foundations of a British tradition of parliamentary socialism in the Labour Party.

Most Marxists would fall into one of the latter two camps, and this division has always been extremely important. One camp's position may be expressed by the social democracy of Eduard Bernstein. He was committed to the education of the working class in advanced industrial society towards voting a mass party into political power by parliamentary means. This 'evolutionary socialism' or 'gradualism' was branded as 'revisionism' (with regard to Marx's work) by Kautsky and then Lenin.

7. E. P. Thompson, *The Making of the English Working Class* (Harmondsworth, 1970).

8. Geraint Williams, 'Introduction' to *John Stuart Mill on Politics and Society* (London, 1976).

9. Speech in Amsterdam, *KMSW*, p. 594.

In the other camp, a small party of professional revolutionaries prepares for the conquest of state power by sudden and probably violent revolution. It is appropriate for non-advanced (or underdeveloped) societies with more despotic or authoritarian governments. Revolutions of the twentieth century have been characterized by this type of social condition and strategy.[10]

The obvious question is, how may so many different types of socialist strategy take the name of Marxism? Why is the situation so confused? Part of the answer, clearly, lies in the different social contexts of each Marxism. But the whole answer must inevitably include reference to Marx's Marxism, indicating both its uniqueness and its openness to ambiguous interpretation.

Marx's Marxism

It is impossible to summarize Marx. One of the last Renaissance men, as David McLellan describes him, he embraced at once the disciplines of history, economics and political science (as well as what is now called sociology), while at the same time retaining a profound interest and delight in classical literature and Shakespeare throughout his life. This, of course, is his great appeal. He offers a total understanding of the world, a way of changing the world, and a view of what the world could be like. Moreover, as we have said, Marxism touches reality at extremely sensitive points. It is, in a sense, a politics of hunger. As C. Wright Mills accurately remarked: 'The work of Marx, taken as a whole, is a savage indictment of one alleged injustice: that the profit, the comfort, the luxury of one man is paid for by the loss, the misery, the denial, of another.'[11]

Let us unpack the preceding statement about Marxism. It is first a world-view ('a total understanding of the world') which stands in opposition to all other world-views. Marx learned from the young Hegelians to criticize religion ('the presupposition of all criticism'[12]) as a prelude to applying Hegel's method to the 'real world' of man. For Hegel had done no better than the theologians, merely substituting the state for God. Marx wanted to show that the state itself embodies a false ideology which stands in the way of human emancipation.

10. John Dunn, *Modern Revolutions* (London, 1974).
11. C. W. Mills, *The Marxists* (Harmondsworth, 1963), p. 35.
12. 'Introduction to Hegel's Philosophy of Right', *KMSW*, p. 63.

So criticism had to begin with religion, which is a projection of human need onto a God-figure, thus leading to a mistaken account of the world. Thus (in Germany, following Feuerbach), 'Criticism has plucked the imaginary flowers from the chains not so that man may bear the chains without any imagination or comfort, but so that he may throw away the chains and pluck living flowers. The criticism of religion disillusions man so that he may think, act, and fashion his own reality as a disillusioned man come to his senses, so that he may revolve around himself as his real sun.'[13] Once the chains are exposed, the solution will become obvious. The flowers are any ideology. Ideology is a product of a particular set of economic relationships. The radical solution to human alienation and exploitation (the chains) is a change at the base-level of economic relationships. The particular set of economic relationships known as capitalism alienates the worker from his product, from the act of production, from his human social essence as *homo faber*, and from his fellow-workers.

The way of changing this situation, argued Marx (to turn to the second point), is through proletarian revolution, '. . . the formation of a class with radical chains . . . the object of no particular injustice but injustice in general . . . In a word it is the complete loss of humanity and can only recover itself by the complete redemption of humanity.'[14] True human destiny, for Marx, lies in the hands of the proletariat (with a little help from its friend the intelligentsia).

But there are two aspects to this. 'Men make their own history, but they do not make it just as they please; they do not make it under circumstances chosen by themselves, but under circumstances directly encountered, given, and transmitted from the past.'[15] There is first the subjective side of human self-creation, especially through class-conscious organization and action. At the right moment, when capitalism is collapsing through its own internal contradictions, the proletariat may make a revolution. Later Marxists, encouraged by Marx's own apparent enthusiasm for catalysing agencies such as the Paris Commune, have used this to justify speeding up the progress to the new world. But Marx also believed that the right circumstances must be awaited before his kind of revolution could take place.

13. *Ibid.* p. 64.
14. *Ibid.* pp. 72-73.
15. '18th Brumaire of Louis Bonaparte', *KMSW*, p. 300.

This, secondly, is the objective side to history. According to observable laws of economic development, history is moving towards communist society. The material conditions of production were decisive for Marx's view of history (and this is what *he* meant by 'materialism'). Just as capitalism had developed out of feudal and mercantile society, so a new set of economic relationships would one day transcend capitalism. Capitalism will outlive its usefulness and, having created a new class on which it depends, will have to give way to its ascendancy. The surplus-value which can be extracted by various means will eventually be exhausted, and a new form of society will emerge.

This is how to change the world. As Andrew Kirk has said, 'We can only marvel at the brilliant synthesis which Marx achieved between man's longing for personal significance and a worth-while cause to live and sacrifice himself for and his hope that science really does possess the key to unlock the enigma of man's contradictions and the power to provoke an unprecedented leap into a qualitatively new era.'[16] But what will the 'new era' be like? How will human or 'communist' society (that which eventually develops after socialism) be different from what we now experience? This is the third attraction of Marxism.

An Alternative Reality

Marx offered an alternative reality to competitive, money-worshipping, unjust, and self-crippling bourgeois life. The 'redemption of humanity' is the culmination of the history of human self-creation through work. All will be free to be themselves. The benefits of capitalist technology will be appropriated for all, and all will have more time to develop themselves as people. At last society will 'inscribe on its banners: from each according to his ability to each according to his needs!'[17] Finally, 'under collective property, the so-called will of the people (the bourgeois state) disappears in order to make way for the real will of the co-operative'.[18] The state will be transcended, along with all class paternalism and superiority. Participation will become a meaningful term.

The final attraction of Marxism is its alleged anti-

16. Andrew Kirk, 'Marxism and the Church in Latin America', in *Missionalia* 6 (1978), and in *Evang. Rev. of Theol.* 3 (1979), pp. 107-118.
17. 'Critique of the Gotha Programme', *KMSW*, p. 569.
18. 'On Bakunin's *Statism and Anarchy*', *KMSW*, p. 563.

utopianism: it is based on an empirical social analysis. Revolution and the new society are concrete possibilities rooted in specific social realities. But this attraction is also one of Marxism's greatest bones of contention. Bernstein denied that Marx's analysis was sociologically adequate, and thus a new kind of praxis was called for. This is what in fact became social democracy. In Britain, this was the stance of Marxist G. D. H. Cole, one of the greatest recent historians of socialism. The social democratic trend is also visible in the Communist Party whose programme, *The British Road to Socialism*, while ostensibly adhering to Marxism-Leninism, is pledged to the parliamentary route to socialism.

Lenin, who in many ways was as 'revisionist' as Bernstein, denied that class and capitalist analysis was sufficient. He substituted 'party' for Marx's 'proletariat' as the engineers, rather than the mere agents, of the revolution. The small élite who seek to seize power by conspiratorial and violent means has been important not only in Russia, but in other predominantly peasant countries such as China and Cuba. In this case, Marx's empirical analysis is supplemented by guerilla action to force early fulfilment of the socialist dream.

Marx's work was both unfinished and ambiguous when he died. Social Democrats and Bolshevik-style revolutionaries have been trying to finish it and make it less ambiguous ever since. For the former, the dream is still in the future. For many heirs of the latter, the dream has become a nightmare.

But it ought to be said that there are Christians who willingly countenance either the social democratic or the revolutionary political styles. They decisively reject aspects of Marxism as a world-view, but accept his analysis and its implications. Míguez Bonino in Argentina calls for a strategic alliance with revolutionary Marxists which may involve Christian participation in the overthrow of oppressive regimes.[19] And Robert Holman, in Britain, who describes himself as a socialist and not a Marxist, nevertheless accepts parts of the Marxist analysis of welfare capitalism, and urges grass-roots collective action to bring about authentic change.[20]

Why Not Marxism?

The conventional evangelical response to Marxism has been

19. *Op. cit.* (n.1 above).
20. Robert Holman, *Poverty: Explanation of Social Deprivation* (Oxford, 1978).

aversion and rejection. Without doubt, the main reason for this has not been an intelligent appreciation and repudiation of Marxism as a world-view, but rather an opposition to regimes which harass and persecute believers. Marx the atheist is discovered via sensationalized stories of atheistic communism's anti-Christian policies (which are usually based on a core of tragic truth). But since the 1970s' reawakening of the evangelical social conscience, Marxism is on the lips of Christians once more. Many seem to be wondering, why not Marxism?

The failure of the fathers to analyse and criticize Marxism from a biblical perspective is now being visited on the children. Ronald Sider, himself a champion of biblical realism in ethics, still has to ask 'Is God a Marxist?' (which is more a reflection of his audience's attitude than his).[21] Marxist analysis appears to many to be a valid adjunct to Christian faith in the social realm. This state of affairs has two roots, ignorance of Marxism and ignorance of the Scriptures — especially in the notorious 'selective hermeneutic' sense.

I believe in the uniqueness and relevance of the Christian gospel and its social implications. There can be no synthesis or symbiosis with Marxism. But I also believe that many issues raised by Marxism are highly pertinent to Christian praxis. The price of ignoring Marxism is minimizing aspects of Christian faith. Briefly, we must ask two questions: what is wrong with capitalism? and what is wrong with Marxism?

Critique of Capitalism

The Christian critique of capitalism exists at two levels. First, there is the challenge to Christian indulgence in luxury goods and comfortable lifestyles, which was reinforced by the realization of a world ecological crisis. John Taylor's incisive *Enough is Enough*,[22] and Ron Sider's *Rich Christians in an Age of Hunger* are examples of this. Secondly, Christian economists have engaged in a biblical critique of the roots of the capitalist ethos and economic system. Examples of this are Donald Hay's *A Christian Critique of Capitalism* and Bob Goudzwaard's *Economic Stewardship versus Capitalist*

21. Ronald Sider, *Rich Christians in an Age of Hunger* (London, 1978).
22. J. V. Taylor, *Enough is Enough* (London, 1975).

Religion.[23] It is no accident that neither level of critique begins with the question, 'What about the workers?'

Goudzwaard, taking a Christian philosophical stance, argues that capitalism is characterized by three things: 'economism', the treating of societal structures like land and labour in terms of their isolated economic aspect without due regard to social and ethical aspects; 'commercialism', where market criteria become all-important and economic values are simply equivalent to market values; lastly, 'competitive dynamism', where there are social constraints to combine values and resources to obtain maximum money profit in a competitive entrepreneurial struggle. All these characteristics are rejected by Goudzwaard in favour of a responsible, pur- posive, Christian understanding of economic life.

Donald Hay, using a more direct exegetical method, proposes a critique of capitalism from the standpoint of a creation ethic. Many of his conclusions are similar to Goudz- waard's, though he uses more theological language. Because capitalism (described both in its 'pure' form and in practice) discourages proper stewardship, which is part of human 'dominion', tends to damage the biblical understanding of work (by accepting unemployment and alienation as in- evitable), and fails to produce a just allocation of resources, especially income, Hay concludes thus: '. . . capitalism, as a system, falls a long way short of satisfying God's creation plan'. And it is no use arguing that it is a 'lesser evil', because 'at its root the philosophical bases of capitalism are opposed to Christian ethics'.

Other aspects of the outworking of capitalism have also stimulated the evangelical conscience in recent years. These especially have to do with the global dimensions of expan- sionism and corresponding economic dependence. (And this, of course, applies equally to state socialist neo-colonialism.) As Jim Wallis succinctly puts it: 'The system of empire is based on the consumer society. . . An international economic system that keeps huge sectors of humanity at a sub-human level while permitting the minority to consume most of the world's resources can only result in conflict.'[24]

And if this American young evangelical sees Christians

23. D. Hay, *A Christian Critique of Capitalism* (Bramcote, Notts., 1975); B. Goudzwaard, *Economic Stewardship versus Capitalist Religion* (Toronto, 1972). See also A. B. Cramp, *Towards a Christian Critique of Secular Economic Theory* (Toronto, 1974); A. Storkey, *A Christian Social Perspective* (Leicester, 1979).
24. Jim Wallis, *Agenda for Biblical People* (New York, 1976), p. 84.

conviving at such a system, Míguez, speaking from Latin America, agrees. He laments the 'quite evident relation between the capitalist colonial and neo-colonial expansion into what is now called the "Third World" and the missionary enterprise'. Unfortunately, however, it is only a short step from this to the acceptance of the analysis and proposed solution (which is confrontationist and potentially violent) of a Marxist like André Gunder Frank. Such a move is logical, especially if one rejects (with Míguez) the possibility of a biblical third way.

Critique of Marxism

To argue for a third way, however, one must first ask the question, if capitalism can be shown in theory and practice to be unbiblical, then what is wrong with the Marxist alternative? I have already stated that there can be no synthesis with Marxism. The reason is that Marxism like capitalism is an outworking of western humanism, and based on a similar notion of progress. At root, it too is opposed to Christian ethics.

Marxism is a challenge because it shames Christians to a rediscovery of an authentic aspect of the Christian task. But Marx believed in the self-redemption of humanity: his way is another religion.

He held a view of personhood (a philosophical anthropology) which is not simply derived from empirical investigation in the modern sense. It is a presupposition which he took from the optimistic humanism of the Enlightenment. He believed in the perfectibility of mankind by unaided effort. For Marx, work makes us human. To be free at work is to be free indeed. Capitalism tends to reduce the labourer to a mere cog in the machine. Marxism exalts him to the status of ideal person.[25] Scripture sees work as a means of expressing our humanity before God. Is this not a third way?

Marx also embraced an understanding of history at variance with biblical faith. He derived it mainly from his philosophical mentor, Hegel. Central to it are the ideas of negation, transcendence and persistence (*Aufhebung*). The eventual outcome of the class-struggle would be the negation of class-struggle and its transcendence in socialism. But this

25. Johan van der Hoeven, *Karl Marx: The Roots of his Thought* (Toronto, 1976), ch. 5 and epilogue.

may be guaranteed only by reference to Marx's new person, thus returned to his or her true humanity, who would be transformed in the new conditions. And if the new person did not emerge? Marx did not countenance this possibility. Countries which have abolished capitalism could find themselves with new classes, new dominant élites. The philosophy of change could be exchanged for a conservative, repressive ideology which nevertheless retains the Marxist tag. Human selfishness could re-establish private accumulation and consumerism even after the official demise of capitalism. The story is all too well known.

It is at this level that the critique of Marxism must begin. Christians may rightly take note of a Marxist analysis of structural injustice, and the social constraints on fulfilled personhood. For Marx does see that economics is an inescapably *social* science, which has inevitably evaluative content. And he discerns the patterns of human domination which are built into the system. But he never goes beyond the structural analysis of humanity's chains. For Marx to concede that people themselves could be wrong — intrinsically misdirected and internally warped — would be to fly in the face of his self-confessed humanism.

One of Marxism's greatest attractions is praxis, that unique combination of theory and practice which has so challenged Christians to 'practise the truth' in recent years. But if it is not the 'truth' which is being practised, it is obviously dangerous from a Christian point of view.

This is why, for all the conscience-pricking work of the theologies of liberation, the question of their stance on Marxism is so critical. Theologies of liberation are ever in danger of being merely 'other gospels', and therefore anathema to Christian praxis.[26] While the liberationists may catalyse the timely development of an evangelical or biblical theology of liberation,[27] its current exponents tend to take too much from Marx and not enough from the Bible.

José Miranda sets out to be an exception to this in his *Marx and the Bible*,[28] where he tries to demonstrate exegetically the central liberative theme of the Scriptures. But while evangelicals have much to learn from the weight of biblical evidence produced for a God of the oppressed, Miranda

26. This is argued by Kenneth Hamilton in C. E. Armerding (ed.), *Evangelicals and Liberation* (Nutley, N.J., 1977), pp. 1-9.
27. Clark Pinnock, 'An Evangelical Theology of Human Liberation', *Sojourners*, Feb.-March 1976.
28. José Miranda, *Marx and the Bible* (London, 1977).

takes this to be the supreme message of Christianity. The oppression-liberation motif, epitomized for him (and others) in the exodus, turns the gospel into a process whereby people are made increasingly free from the law. His argument is directed against the enslavement of Christianity to the Greek elevation of permanence and law above change and freedom.

Although his attempt is more biblically-based than some others, he tries to fit everything into the oppression-liberation theme. No wonder 'law' and 'permanence' have such low premium for him. Once liberation-oppression is the interpretative key, the affinities with Marxist humanism become very clear. As Alfredo Fierro puts it, '. . . more and more people are professing to be both Christians and Marxists. This confronts them with the task of elaborating a theology in line with what they now profess.'[29]

Challenge of Liberationists

There are perhaps three key areas of debate raised by the liberationists: the *context* of Christian faith, the *content* of the gospel, and the nature of Christian *commitment*.

Related to Marx's critique of ideologies is the notion of *contextualization*. It is the recognition that all theology is done in a specific socio-cultural milieu, which affects the product. Thus all liberationists deplore the unthinking Christianity-capitalism link, and plead with Gutierrez for 'sinking roots where the pulse of history is beating at this moment and illuminating history with the Word of the Lord of history. . . '[30] It leads, as he says, to a '*new way* to do theology' which not only reflects on the world (sic) but 'rather tries to be part of the process through which the world is transformed'. While this is in some ways commendable as an alternative to the abstract and culture-bound product of some 'theologies', two dangers exist. One is that reflection on *God* can be minimized, and the other that one determining cultural context will simply be exchanged for another.

Secondly, taking the context of theologizing seriously implies that the *content* of the gospel must also be re-examined. Does it relate to personal salvation through the death of Christ, or to the redemption of social structures, or both? May one talk of 'political evangelism' or are there rather

29. Alfredo Fierro, *The Militant Gospel* (London, 1977), p. xiii.
30. Gustav Gutierrez, *A Theology of Liberation* (London, 1974), p. 15.

political *implications* which flow from the gospel? Ron Sider has clarified some of these issues for us, arguing that the language of 'evangelism', 'salvation' and 'redemption' is not appropriate for social action.[31] But this is not an argument for a dualism of evangelism and social action. There is a wholeness in Christ's commission to 'make disciples of all nations . . . teaching them to obey everything I have commanded you' (Matt. 28:19,20). The danger, again, is that of over-reaction to individualism and a-politicism which ends in an equally unbiblical form of socialism and a merely political gospel.

On this hinges the question of Christian *commitment*. From the Marx-inspired concern with praxis (which as Míguez convincingly demonstrates has biblical analogues[32]) comes a renewed emphasis on Christian practice of the truth as well as its defence. This is part of the *'new way* to do theology'. For Gutierrez, theology is 'critical reflection on historical praxis' and is committed to the building of a new, just and fraternal society'.[33] Again, while this may deepen Christian concern for authentic and radical discipleship of Jesus Christ, it could take other directions. The gospel that begins with Marxist alienation and exploitation in Christian dress, ends with a hope only in self-made people re-creating the world as it seems right in their own eyes, and calling it the kingdom of God.

Let us summarize what has been said so far. Marxism's challenge comes at several levels. It is a radical, comprehensive, critique of things as they are which demands an alternative praxis; radical, in that a structural social and historical analysis questions not only the workings of the system, but whether the system itself is human, and comprehensive, in that a total understanding of the world is offered, so that today's Marxists have an interpretation for many events outside the industrial shop-floor itself. The critique which shatters illusions about the benevolence of a capitalist *status quo* is based on a view of ideal person and an alternative society. Lastly, the praxis is a way of actively changing the world, in which neither abstract theory nor mindless activism rule; rather, theory and practice are dynamically intertwined.

31. R. Sider and J. Stott, *Evangelism and Social Justice* (Bramcote, Notts., 1976).
32. *Op. cit.* (n.1 above).
33. Gutierrez, *op. cit.* p. 15.

We have hinted at three separate aspects of a Christian response to Marxism. These may be spelt out as follows. First, humility. Marxism is a human response to Christian failure to practise the truth in every sphere. It highlights the deficiencies of Christian commitment. Secondly, deep disquiet about the roots of Marxism. Human self-redemption is the core of its optimistic gospel. *Homo faber* creates himself through work, deliberately rejecting all 'alienating' reference to power or guidance outside himelf. Marx could not be consistent here, however, and surrogate religious motifs and scarcely-veiled dogmatic judgements abound in his work. It goes without saying that the powers of evil may easily use such a system.

The third aspect of a Christian response has to do with Marxism's historical record. We have every right, on Marx's own terms, to ask why state-socialist societies have failed to fulfil their attractive promises. What we see today in state socialism is the fruit of human autonomy. Marxism emphatically does not mean bureaucratic collectivism, but Marx never suggested how such an outcome could be avoided. He saw many things. But his blind spots have proved to be fatal. His radicalism is not deep enough. His apparently comprehensive range is limited. His critique is grounded in an incomplete view of personhood and an all-too-sketchy outline of ideal society, quite detached from the creator's life-patterns for freedom. Hence he failed both to plumb the depths of alienation (as estrangement from God) and to follow the perfect orthopraxis of the creator's Son. Instead, he bequeathed to an unjust world a powerful locomotive of revolutionary activism, but only the most frail of ethical tracks to run it on.

Beyond Conformism and Confrontationism

The Christian alternative to Marxism must begin with the distinctive and authoritative message of the biblical Scriptures, that to be fully human is to be right with God our maker. Sinful rebellion against God and his ways is the fundamental alienation. At the same time, Christians should be aware of *how* this alienation is manifesting itself in contemporary social situations. Christian faith hinges on the death of sin-bearing Christ. As Andrew Kirk has rightly stressed, a personal discovery and knowledge of God, who is

the *go'el* of the poor and oppressed, is the beginning of true
Christian obedience. Unless Jesus Christ of Nazareth is the
focus of faith and the pattern of discipleship, any claims to
authentic Christian life are hollow.

There is a need to go beyond all conformism to this-worldly
patterns (especially those known to us as western Christians
in capitalist countries) *and* beyond the mere confrontationism
of revolutionary Marxism. This is not the way of Christ. The
Christian social ethic, needed so desperately in our generation, must transcend both capitulation to capitalist logic and
life-styles, *and* power-struggle belligerence and hatred without
sacrificing the biblical ideals of truth and justice found in
Christ. I believe that Christian discipleship entails concern
for the development of a social ethic of this type.

Not being a trained ethicist, I hesitate to go further,
especially as I fear that to do so would open a whole can of
worms. But if the challenge of Marxism is genuinely to be
faced, I must outline what I see as a Christian alternative.
Clearly, there is considerable debate as to the basis of ethics
among Evangelicals. Some plump for creation, others for the
kingdom. Yet others, more speculatively, find the Trinity, incarnation, exodus or *shalom* to be a foundation.

It seems to me, however, that the *whole* biblical message
may be brought to bear on the ethical task. (Richard Mouw's
Politics and the Biblical Drama[34] confirmed my belief that
this is an appropriate method.) Life before God is seen in the
biblical drama as creation, fall, redemption and the future
age (or final kingdom). Each aspect has an important bearing
on what God requires of his people. Each relates to and in-
teracts with the other. We shall glance at them in turn, also
referring to themes already discussed as 'the challenge of
Marxism'.

Creation

First, God's original and ongoing intentions for humankind
are seen most clearly in the creation. A. N. Triton is right
when he argues that behind the Mosaic law, and behind
Jesus' Sermon on the Mount is the creation ideal. 'These con-
stitute the warp and woof of the biblical picture of society as
it was meant to be. Even prior to the entrance of evil there
were structures and positive commands given to man to guide

34. Richard Mouw, *Politics and the Biblical Drama* (Grand Rapids, 1976).

him.'[35] This reference back to the beginning is a legitimate starting point for ethics, primarily because it is Jesus' way. Moreover, it links in with Jesus' dynamic teaching on the kingdom, which in many ways unifies the four motifs under discussion.

Applied to our particular topic, Marxism, the creation ideal[36] explodes the myth of human identity as *homo faber*. The human person is *imago Dei*. This totally different philosophical anthropology is the base line for the development of a purposive Christian social perspective. To quote Mouw, 'Social relationships (are) a central dimension of human nature from a biblical perspective . . . human beings were created for positive social co-operation with each other, to perform certain tasks with respect to the rest of creation, in obedience to the will of the Creator. It is not just that human beings were created to be social, but that they were meant to be social in certain *ways*.'[37]

The development of such a systematic social perspective, which begins with the creation, is both realistic and relevant. Just as creation references are woven into the whole biblical drama, so the whole biblical teaching on the creation must be woven into the Christian social perspective. Donald Hay's critique of capitalism, which begins with the creation pattern of stewardship, work, and so on, is a model. Until Christians follow leads like that, Christian ethics will be adrift in a stormy and hostile seascape, without the identity of port-of-origin.

Fall

Secondly, the entry of sin at the fall must be taken into account as the dimensions of the ethical task are spelled out. From seeing that God had given them 'all things richly to enjoy' in Eden, Adam and Eve were deceived into asserting their own autonomy, and accepting false definitions of life's purpose. They rebelled against the creator, thus initiating the selfish and self-destructive way of idolatry. They trusted their own way and each other above the way of God and God himself.

35. A. N. Triton, *Salt to the World* (Leicester, 1978), p. 35.
36. The phrase 'created order' is all too easily linked with 'law and order', which has connotations I do not intend.
37. Mouw, *op. cit.* p. 28.

This teaches us that as post-fall humans we are always susceptible to distorted thinking and twisted lifestyles. This is why Paul solemnly warns Christians not to be conformed to the pattern of this world, but to be transformed by mind-renewal (Rom. 12:2). The purposive social theory developed from the creation perspective now takes on a critical dimension. The false definitions of reality and false dominions over others must be unmasked by a truly radical critical social analysis.

We may expect inhuman situations to emerge wherever an uncreaturely perspective is dominant in society. If it is alleged that man's chief end is to consume, or to re-make himself through work, life-patterns will be distorted and idolatrous. But if the Eden-exodus teaches us anything, it is that sin is subtle. We may expect unwitting collusion in sinful structures. We may also expect that some will be lured into an uncritical Marxist mind-set. But if Christians are being totally transformed by the Spirit's mind-renewal, then we should be willing to unmask even our own unknowing complicity in sinful life-patterns.

Marxism challenges us deeply here. We need to develop a critical social analysis and practice which is willing honestly to face issues such as: the injustice of an economically stratified society, and the power of the holders of resources (for example, via the media and the Welfare State) over those who are weak; the courageous stand for righteousness in public places alongside the almost total silence from Christians whose capitalist societies systematically exploit and keep in dependence Third World countries by their 'aid programmes'; the alliance of the so-called Protestant work ethic with a system which either deliberately allows for a large pool of unemployment, or else ensures that the benefits of labour accrue not to the labourer, but to his hirer. Biblical critical theory strikes at the very sensitive roots of sin.

Redemption

Thirdly, we turn to redemption. Those who are redeemed, in the biblical sense, are the people of God. As the church in the world, these people have a complex task to perform. Without quibbling over the relative importance of one aspect of the task over another (though it is worth saying emphatically that evangelism is different from social action), particular responsibilities of the church may be mentioned.

While it is confusing and misleading to identify the kingdom of God or redemption with anyone who does not consciously acknowledge the lordship of Jesus Christ, there is a sense in which the church is a 'signpost' of the coming kingdom of Christ.[38] We must distinguish carefully between what R. B. Kuiper refers to as the kingdom of Christ's power and the kingdom of his grace. For example, as the church practises the abolition of ethnic and economic barriers so it may look forward to the time when the curse will be finally reversed, and the whole creation set free from sin and its consequences.

But the task of the church is to be a fellowship of those in Christ, where worship and discipling according to Christ's teaching go on. This cannot but relate to the gospel preached by the church. There is an insidious 'easy-believism' which continues to pervade Evangelicalism. This simultaneously underplays the sovereignty of God in calling out his people, and their responsibility to count the cost of being disciples of Jesus. The cost may involve family difficulties, the forsaking of work which is clearly wrong (as in the instructive case of Zaccheus) and some very painful rethinking of life's purposes, social connections and priorities.

On the one hand, the life-style of believers must be distinctively Christian if we are to be the salt of the earth. Houses, cars, eating habits, children's education, holidays, all these come under the confession, 'Jesus Christ is Lord'. Free enterprise capitalist society produces 'fetishism of commodities' as Marx rightly noted. Christians must actively demonstrate that 'a man's (or a woman's) life does not consist in the abundance of his possessions'. This involves an alternative life-style.

On the other hand, Christians must be seen to have a concern for justice, compatible with Christ's 'positive discrimination' on behalf of the 'wretched of the earth' of his day. This has to operate both at local level and also in attitudes to global justice. Rather like ancient Sodom we 'have surfeit of good and prosperous ease, but do not aid the poor and needy' (Jer. 16:49). Bearing the purposive perspective and critical social analysis in mind, we must corporately work out our economic and political responsibilities in these public spheres.[39]

38. C. Sugden, *Social Gospel or No Gospel?* (Bramcote, Notts., 1977), p. 17.
39. This is likely to differ from person to person and from place to place.

The extent to which the local church can do this, and its relationship to other institutions such as study groups or Christian companies is a matter for debate. The point is that discipleship of Jesus Christ is both radical and communal. If Christ's lordship is not worked out in the proclamation, defence, and practice of the gospel *in the church*, it will not be worked out anywhere.

Final Age

Lastly, the biblical drama builds up to the final age. We have already noted that the church is a pointer to this age. It is the time of fulfilment of all God's purposes and intentions in creation and redemption. Jesus taught his people to pray, 'Your kingdom come, your will be done on earth as it is in heaven'. This aim and goal is also suggestive for a Christian social ethic, especially as it highlights the pitiful deficiency of the Marxist ethic.

Eschatology is a great corrective and stimulus to the ethical task. It is a corrective insofar as we are reminded of an eternal perspective. Ethics can force the eyes down to earth. Eschatology reminds us to lift our eyes to the place from which our help comes. Calvin was as strong on the point that our earthly life is to be shaped by the desire for life eternal as he was in his insistence that our knowledge of ourselves is inextricably connected with our knowledge of God our maker.

But eschatology is also a stimulus in that it reminds us of ideals, and gives ground for a kind of utopian thinking. It allows for genuine hope to be articulated (as opposed to the impotent hope of Marxist or capitalist humanism in man's unaided efforts). But as Míguez perceptively notes, it also means that ethics is continually indispensable. Evil and conflict will be with us until the end of time. Over against the Marxist tendency to suspend ethics for the sake of the revolution or the party, the Christian insists that 'no human class, group, or generation can be considered as merely instrumental'.[40] This utopian thinking must ever be yoked with the purposive perspective and critical social analysis, but essentially it is promoted by the kingdom-vision.

Utopian thinking may be particularized in a social-political programme, but it must never be imagined that a programme

40. *Op. cit.* p. 129.

is enough. We need the ideals in order mentally to transcend the *status quo*, but they must be a sign *within* the situation. We must focus on specific areas of failure (in terms of the biblical ideal) and struggle to right those wrongs. There will, therefore, always be a concern among God's people for the poor and disadvantaged. This is what I understand by the term 'biblical realism'.

Whether or not we share Alan Storkey's vision of a Christian political party for Britain, Christians should be indebted to him for his insightful analysis of contemporary politics. Here is someone who has dared to think realistically through economic life, the education system, the penal system, health and welfare, and so on, with a view to articulating a new politics. I shall do no more than refer readers to this analysis.[41] Many would like me to go further at this point, but it would not be proper. If what I have written is right, then it is incumbent not merely upon isolated individuals like me to suggest ways forward. Rather it should be the task of groups within the Christian community to work out the implications of what I have said in practical detail. I reject the lust for instant answers in this complex and confusing area.

But I do wish to make two final brief points. Eschatology produces a concern for change. Christians have been paralysed by *status quoism* for so long that they have come to believe in it. The hope of God's purposes being finally fulfilled catalyses desire for change in accordance with his word. But this implies that politics be taken seriously. Probably due to the black and white nature of traditional Christian teaching, Christians have often been unwilling to enter the area of political decisions and compromises. But this leaves the door wide open for the anti-political activity of many Marxists who believe in confrontation and struggle as means to achieve power. The concern for justice and reconciliation on God's terms is thus muted in public life.

To the challenge of Marxism must come a response which is rooted in God's whole word to the whole of human life before him. Though Marxism confronts us with our Christian failures, it is in the better way of the Lord Jesus Christ that we find a totally different framework for a radically different praxis, or wisdom. That way starts and continues with a cross.

41. Alan Storkey, 'A Christian Party Manifesto', *Third Way* 2:12 (1978).

Reading List

José Míguez Bonino, *Christians and Marxists: the Mutual Challenge to Revolution* (London, 1976).
Johan van der Hoeven, *Karl Marx: The Roots of his Thought* (Toronto, 1976).
Alan Storkey, *A Christian Social Perspective* (Leicester, 1979).
Andrew Kirk, 'The Meaning of Man in the debate between Christianity and Marxism' *Themelios* 1:2-3 (1976).
Bernard Zylstra, 'Karl Marx: Radical Humanist', *Vanguard*, Dec. 1973.
David Lyon, 'Approaching Marx', *Third Way* 1:19 (1977).
David Lyon, *Karl Marx: A Christian Appreciation of his Life and Thought* (Tring, Herts., 1979).

Questions for Discussion

1   Have evangelical Christians too readily allowed the atheism of Marxism and the anti-Christian policies of Communist regimes to blind them to its challenge and relevance?

2   Consider Marx's claim that religion like an opiate has induced passive submission to the harsh injustice of life. How far is it true that evangelical Christianity has steeled Christians to *endure* what they should have been seeking to *reform,* to prefer peace (the absence of conflict) rather than campaign for justice?

3   Are there any reasons why Christians should not accept the validity of the Marxist critique of capitalism?

4   'Marxism is a human response to Christian failure to practise the truth in every sphere.' What are the implications of this assessment?

*I understood my brief for the Social Ethics Conference to require chiefly an exposition of Marxism's salient features, especially as it *challenges* Christian commitment. The paper is printed almost exactly as delivered, and thus remains at the level of generality which seemed appropriate for the Conference. It needs to be filled out with concrete examples.

KMSW refers to *Karl Marx: Selected Writings,* ed. D. McLellan (London, 1977).

Chapter Six
Man in Society
E. David Cook

CHAPTER SIX

Man in Society

THE PHILOSOPHY STUDENT SOON LEARNS THAT TRUE philosophy is all about metaphysics. Metaphysics, whatever that is, asks the nitty-gritty questions. What is true? What is there? How do we know? The second thing we learn is that every philosophy rests on a presuppositional framework. We all need a point from which to lever the world. That basic framework presupposes crucial things in epistemology and ontology. Before we can give a description of the world and our views concerning the nature of things we must make assumptions about what there is, what we can and do know and what constitutes truth and falsity. The real interest concerning epistemology and ontology comes to a head in political and religious terms with the particular anthropology each view holds. Too rarely do we examine the anthropology of the great ideologies which are competing for our attention in the twentieth century. What is man? How are we to understand him and his nature?

Behaviourism and Existentialism

The modern tendency, particularly evidenced in sociology and anthropology, is to adopt the observer viewpoint. The sociologist stands on the side-lines and watches the game in progress. His task is purely descriptive. He describes the phenomena. His special delight is to concentrate on people's behaviour. What they do matters more than what they say or are in themselves. (I am reminded of a philosophical graffito in Keele University: 'To be is to do — existentialism. To do is to be — behaviourism. Do be do be do — Sinatra.') Man is interpreted as his behaviour. Behind this lie particular materialistic presuppositions which are reductionist in flavour. Man is reduced from any psycho-spiritual, physical unity to the level of the purely physical, be that chemical or biological. Man is seen as simply a machine and society interpreted as a social mechanism.

This reductionism has evoked an equal and opposite force in reaction. 'I am a human being. Do not fold, mutilate or shred.' The anti-mechanism, anti-behaviourism views find their most natural expression in literary and artistic settings. Existentialist drama reveals this reaction at the other extreme where attention is fastened on specific moments of human experience in which the internal experience is the key to any understanding. This is what makes existentialism such a difficult philosophy to grasp. In a sense it cannot be stated, it can only be shown. Thus the existentialist novelist, dramatist and artist do not so much propound a philosophical stance, as present us with situations where we are called on to enter not only imaginatively but in reality into the absurdity, pointlessness and lack of meaning which is the human lot. Man is what he experiences and particularly what he wills. The sum of man is his choices.[1]

The existentialist position also reduces to phenomenology, where the facts of inner experience are examined and re-experienced, but rather than this leading to objectivity it leads to the opposite, subjectivity, whether we take the observer viewpoint or the participating position. Both extremes seem to be at fault, for there is a much more complex, yet dynamic interaction between subjectivity and objectivity which modern science is leading us towards and which we need to grasp in every area of study, not least in theology.

The Christian then comes to a society and culture which in fact have contradictory views of the nature of man. Man is simply matter. Man is purely biological. Man is purely the product of his conditioning. Man is what his society makes him. Man is the sum of his behaviour. Man is what he feels and wills. Man is . . . The Christian view of man seems to be

1. For a fuller account see *Blind Alley Beliefs* (Glasgow, 1979), by the present writer.

no more than and accordingly no less than an alternative to these views. Ideally we should proceed as follows.

Given a number of competing theories as to the nature of man there must be a procedure for deciding between them. This entails looking at each view in turn. The examination would take the following form. First, we would be seeking to discern the inner logic of each view. We would be trying to test each view for internal coherence and self-consistency. Given that it was consistent and not self-contradictory we would then move to the next level of analysis. Secondly, we would wish to test each view as to its correspondence with reality and the facts. This is more difficult for most views actually offer some definition of what constitutes the facts, but the point and test must still stand in the sense that each view must be seen to match up with reality and not to contradict what we experience, discover and are confronted by in the world and society. Given this correspondence test, we are then, and only then, in a position truly to compare and contrast alternative views.

The basis of judgement between competing views must rest on which offers the best sort of explanation in either completeness or economy and neatness — which is a version of Occam's Razor. There is a third kind of test between alternatives, that of fertility in creating new ideas and bringing about creativity.[2] This stems from the application of relativity theory to research and epistemology.

As Christians it is essential that in both apologetics and ethics we take alternative views very seriously, especially those which have a large following in our culture. To take them seriously means to seek to understand and then criticize them along the lines suggested. Such examinations are outwith the scope of my present paper, but the analysis of the Marxist challenge[3] is the kind of thing I have in mind. I rather wish to turn our attention to the other horn of the dilemma I raised, the nature of biblical anthropology. Before we are able to develop a proper relation between biblical anthropology and the many differing cultural expressions of the nature of man we must be clear about the nature of man as outlined in Scripture.

My aim will be to give an overview of the doctrine of man, bearing in mind the bases and contents of alternative views and accordingly seeking to highlight the points of contact.

2. See T. F. Torrance, *Theological Science* (Oxford, 1969).
3. See chapter five.

These points may be used in positive and negative ways. They may be seen as a common basis for discussion and joint projects as has been the case with some Christian-Marxist dialogue and its expression in liberation theology in the South American setting. Alternatively, the points of contact may rather become sticking points at which fundamental decisions must be taken to discern the truth of one view and falsity of another.

Given the backdrop of a biblical anthropology, I wish then to turn our attention to three key social issues which, I believe, have far-reaching implications in ethical, political, and social policy terms. These are individualism and collectivism, sex, and race. My aim in this section will be simply to draw attention to the nature of the issues and to suggest some dangers to be avoided and avenues to be pursued. In the final section I wish to develop briefly four areas where the strengths of traditional Evangelicalism need to be applied to our culture along with a parallel awareness of Evangelicalism's own inadequacies and weaknesses.

The Biblical Doctrine of Man

Traditionally there are two great starting points for the development of a biblical anthropology. Oliver O'Donovan described these as creation and kingdom.[4] The first starts at the beginning and develops the doctrine of man along the lines of progression from creation and all that it entails. We shall see where this leads us. The alternative is to begin with the revelation of man at his best and this must mean beginning with the person of Christ, the perfect man. Having seen the ideal we can then understand how far short mankind falls of God's perfect standard. For the sake of completeness we shall utilize both approaches.

Image and Dust

The creation-centred approach may be summed up in the word *image*. The idea of the image of God has formed the basis for many theological positions from Irenaeus through Schleiermacher to Brunner. Man is made in the image of

4. See chapter one.

God. In this way man is both a representation and a representative. He cannot be understood only by reference to himself. This is the rock on which the modern subjectivist tendencies within and without theology must shatter. Man is not truly self-referent. To understand his nature fully we must be able to refer to the original, to that which is represented in man.

What is more tendentious however is the actual content which we may attach to the notion of 'image'. Are we simply dealing with certain *formal* characteristics of man, or are there specific *qualities* which may be discerned? Brunner, for example, draws the distinction between man having the form of God but not having the content.[5] The formal image of God in man is responsibility and answerability. The content, which man lacks, is being in love. Thus man is confronted with the demand to take responsibility in loving his fellow man, himself and God, but lacks the ability to be a 'lover'. It is not my intention to seek to explicate the meaning of the term image, for there is exceedingly little in Scripture to go on. Rather I want to take the bald statement of man being in the image of God and see what implications we may legitimately derive from the Bible.

The first main theme is that man is made in God's image not because man chooses to be but because God makes man thus. We are created beings. We are not free to be whatever we wish to be or would like to be. We are God's creatures and that must imply certain limits as to what man is able to do and to be. Perhaps one of the key limits is that of freedom, or in more traditional philosophical language, that of autonomy. Is man free to make his own laws and to live his life in anyway he pleases? The Christian answer must be negative. Man may try to live without reference to God and even try to assume responsibility for himself, but he cannot escape from his maker and his created being. He does not have infinite possibilities for change bound up in himself. Man is limited.

Given man's created nature, it is crucial for man to understand his limits both in physical and psychological terms, but also in social and spiritual areas too. Some human experiments are bound to fail, given the nature of man. If we examine some of the areas of breakdown in terms of individual and social collapse we may see some of the limits of man and thus be able to define what he is, by seeing what he cannot be and do.

5. E. Brunner, *Man in Revolt,* (London, 1942).

Rationality and Personality

Theologians have tried to express the content of man's image of God along the lines of rationality and personality. To illustrate the first we turn to science. The scientist begins the business of scientific research making two assumptions. The first is that there is something there to be understood and the second that he will be able to understand it. He assumes a basic rationality in the nature of things and in himself. If God is the creator it is reasonable to suppose that things have a purpose and order. Hence for centuries science and theology went hand in hand. To study God was to study the nature of things in their ultimate rationality. If we are made in the image of God we share in his rationality. I do not myself think that this means that we are all highly intelligent, but rather that it is the level of rationality which marks off sanity from insanity, the child from the adult, humanity from animality. This is crucial for our understanding of man in society. If we are fundamentally rational beings, there is the possibility of argument, discussion, reasoning, justification, evidence and science. Without such rationality, there seems no genuine basis for communication, understanding, joint-functioning, informed choice, evangelism, or apologetic. How we treat people and how we educate our children and how we expand the frontiers of knowledge all rest on rationality. The alternative is irrationalism and chaos, offering no hope of understanding God, ourselves or our world.

The other theme is that of personality. What is the real person? Is it the physical body we all see and identify as Tom Jones? Or is the real Tom lurking somewhere inside? Peter Sarstedt expressed it thus: 'Where do you go to my lovely, when you're alone in your bed? Tell me the thoughts that surround you. I want to look inside your head.' Some suggest that the real I and the real you is our inner being, our spirit, our soul. For some this is described by God breathing his life within us. What seems crucial for biblical anthropology is that man is more than his body and more than his mind. We must not start with a divided self or person, for we can never then put the pieces together. Rather we must see man as a psycho-somatic unity. Our society must then deal with the whole person — physical, mental and spiritual. Any ordering of society which ignores aspects of man's being is destined to cause harm and to be not only destructive but self-destructive. In terms of our social policies, or our church programmes, are we truly dealing with the whole person?

Where the breakdown most obviously occurs is in the realm of work. It is no surprise that *Which?* discovered that clergy are the poorest paid but most satisfied of all workers, particularly at the professional level. God gave man work to do. If man does that work properly then he pleases God. That is he worships God by responding properly to God. We may illustrate this by considering man's unity with nature and yet his difference from it.[6]

Man and Nature

Links between man and nature are obvious in the common biological and chemical make-up which man shares with the animal world. He is dust and to dust he must return. But man's unity with nature does not imply identity. Some ecologists adopt a Buddhist-type approach which sees man and nature as basically one. This view tends to glorify, romanticize and even to deify nature. Unacceptable conclusions follow: if nature is beyond detraction it must be accepted warts and all. But it is not always benevolent and a view which encourages its uncritical acceptance must quickly degenerate into a fatalism which accepts whatever happens as good and right. Furthermore it reduces man to the level of grass, though there does appear to be a difference between man thinking he is the same as grass, and grass thinking that man is the same as grass.

Man differs from nature. Though man is part of his environment, he is distinguishable from it. In thought he can disengage from his surroundings, can ask and answer questions and act accordingly. Between man and his environment there is a basic, qualitative distinction. To say this is not to be arrogant, but rather to state the obvious.

In the creation story man is distinguished from nature in several ways. He is the climax of God's work: only when he is included in the now completed creative process is creation pronounced to be very good. Man is made in the image of God. Therefore his function in nature is unique. God gives him an injunction: he is told to multiply, to subdue the earth and to have dominion over the animal realm.

In fulfilling this commission man has been guilty of abuse.

6. See E. D. Cook, 'Some Theological Implications for Ecology', *Faith and Thought* 102 (1975), pp. 184-196.

He has too often become parasitical on nature and deified himself. But in exercising dominion, is it necessary for man to be aggressive? Part of the problem is that the words 'dominion' and 'subdue' can be suggestive of aggressiveness. Yet they have other connotations too, e.g. of the rule of a king over a people or a master over a servant. Dominion need not imply domination; certainly it does not imply extermination. A balance is possible between creatureliness and dominion. The biblical picture is of the shepherd-king who cares for and protects his flock. This is the model for man. One expression of this role is seen in the naming of the animals. Control over the name implies control over the named object, but man's giving of the names, although it implies power, is a loving, gentle act almost paralleled by our use of private nicknames for those we love.

The pre-fall situation ought not to be the main focus of attention in understanding man's difference from the rest of creation. It is rather to the flood narrative that attention must be drawn. It is in the renewal of a covenant with man that God describes the situation of our fallen world. In Genesis 9 we find the beginnings of fear and dread on the part of animals towards man. Animal flesh is now, for the first time, at man's disposal as a food supply. After the flood, there is a clear and violent separation of man from the animal world.

The Bible now pictures man as a rebel. He is selfish, self-centred and sinful. Through the fall he becomes a tyrant over nature. The ecological crisis is one fruit of that sin. It is to be doubted whether man can ever totally overcome the results of his sin and disobedience in relation to the natural realm, until he is totally redeemed. If so, it is only proximate cures we can hope for rather than absolute ones. For the Christian in society this may result in questions as to how best to use his energy and time. Should he first seek to change men recognizing that it is the changed man who has the potential for God-like relationships with creation? Or should he seek to alleviate the situation by other means which would involve a realistic assessment of man's condition and hence the recognition that man's attitude to his environment will be changed only by appeal to selfish motives?[7]

It is important to note that the final difference between man and nature is not so much in status as in function. Man is called to be a manager, trustee, steward or vice-regent. On God's mandate, he is entitled to live from the estate, but that

7. See chapters three and seven.

does not mean he owns it. It is held in trust for his Lord, to whom he is answerable; he will be called to give an account of his stewardship. Yet this is no mere business relationship, but one of love in which man is seen as a co-worker with God. This work is not to be characterized by a 'laissez-faire' attitude. A good manager is involved in research and development for his master, remembering that the shepherd-king is his model and that the sheep matter. In the parable of the talents in Matthew 25, it is the developer who is rewarded and not the conservationist. This is no charter for exploitation, for the gain was in no way selfish, but all part of fulfilment of stewardship. The conservationist made no attempt to put his resources to their proper use and so reaped the unpleasant consequences.

Man is one with nature — yet different from it — in the work he has been given to do. At the same time it was not good for man to be alone. Man on his own lacked something so God created man in society. If the well-being of man is to be any kind of criterion, man is necessarily a social being. Some have seen in this a reflection of the Trinitarian nature of the Godhead. The Father, Son and Spirit live in community in which there is unity yet difference. Man is to reflect even that aspect of the Godhead — unity in difference and difference in unity. The history of salvation has reinforced this point. It is the people of Israel who are in communion or out of it with God. The sin of one, for example Achan, affects the whole. This same community is part and parcel of the New Testament with the emergence of the church, the new people of God. This raises questions as to which social setting is basic and crucial for our view of anthropology, but before we come to that we must sum up this section.

Man is made from the dust of the earth in the image of God. As dust and image he is created. He has the likeness of God but is not God himself. He has a purpose and a task to fulfil set in the context of a community no matter how basic. What we have not stressed is the fallenness of man. It is part of the weakness of the image approach that it necessarily plays down the fall, yet cannot deny it all together. The least it can say is that man is not what he ought to be. In one sense that is enough for us. Man is not only created, he is also not now as he ought to be. He falls short of the glory of God. He does not fulfil the image of God. The marks of fallenness are everywhere. Even the Marxist makes them clear. He stresses man's inhumanity to man, man's inhumanity to the created order, to nature itself, and man's inability to live with himself in any kind of harmony and peace. Sin has marred the image, but to what extent? Is it a fatal shattering, or is there enough of that image left to build a new society? Man is dust — but he is also destined for glory.

Incarnation and Glory

The second key approach to a biblical anthropology must be more briefly treated. It centres on the incarnation, the revelation of Christ. One effect of the publication of *The Myth of God Incarnate*[8] has been to make the whole church ask what difference if any the incarnation makes. Is the incarnation fundamental to Christianity or not? What kind of faith is left if we remove the divinity of Christ? A truly biblical anthropology reveals man not only as he is, but also as he may be. This is where the incarnation becomes the starting point for anthropology. We can understand man properly only if we see him as he should be. 'Veiled in flesh the Godhead see, Hail the incarnate deity, Pleased as man with man to dwell, Jesus our Immanuel' — God with us. In one crucial sense this reduces God to a size and shape that humanity can grasp. God is in Christ tangible, comprehensible, knowable. And yet the tantalizing thing about Christ is that the more we seem to get to know him, the less we really appear to understand. We *apprehend* something of God, but we do not *comprehend* him in the sense of fully grasping and knowing him.

If there is any doubt about the goodness of matter, then the incarnation shows again that matter is not in itself evil. This enables the possibility which becomes actuality in Christ, that humanity need not be defeated by sin. The biblical picture is one of man struggling; Paul expresses it as the flesh striving against the spirit. In Christ we see the victory over the flesh, the world and the devil. The human is still human, but it is what true humanness was created to be. The 'very God and very man' of the reformed catechisms draws our attention again and again to the true divinity and true humanity of Christ. If he is less than divine we are no better off, for he cannot help our predicament. If he is more than human he has an unfair advantage and offers real man no hope in this world of coping with the flesh and the devil. This is the key way in which the transcendent becomes immanent. Either

8. *The Myth of God Incarnate*, ed. J. Hick (London, 1977).

alone is useless. The totally transcendent God is too distant from man to make any difference, the totally immanent God is too near man to be able to change his basic condition. Thus a point of intersection between the transcendent and the immanent is required and that is Christ who is fully both and exclusively neither.

In the model of Christ we have the revelation of the glory of God and at the same time the revelation of the glory of man. In Christ, man is truly man. Thus the anthropology of the Christian is rooted in the *indwelling Christ* — Christ indwelling and indwelling in Christ. Man finds his fullness in Christ. That is where we are the new creation and old things are passed away.

The process of redemption and renewal is that of glorification. We are being transformed from one degree of glory to another. Christ in us is the hope of glory and in the Spirit we are already partakers of his glory. Christ then is the perfect standard for man. By his life and by his death he enables man to attain that standard, that glory, that perfect humanity. But when? Here and now? Or in the eschaton? Or partly now and partly later?

Here we are brought back to the fall and to the real force of redemption. Is the fall still effective? Has the prince of the air still his power? Are we still sinners? Or is Christ's victory real, total and absolute? The usual response is that we are in the middle. D-day happened at the cross where the decisive action was fought once for all and the real victory won. V-day has yet to come when the whole business will be finally tidied up. We are at present engaged in the mopping-up operations. The enemy has no real power but there are still pockets of resistance which need to be wiped out. V-day arrives when Christ returns again in glory, with glory. Then we shall be totally redeemed, our bodies shall be transformed and the whole of creation fundamentally restored, and we shall be like him, for we shall see him as he is.

Now these pictures of dust and glory as the basic and true nature of man are very fine and surely biblical — but how does this help us? If we have passed the evangelical litmus test, we are still left with two different men in society.

Two Societies, One Humanity

The first society is all of humanity, equally created, equally

human, equally fallen. Here is man in society, man in a mess
and man trying by a wide variety of means to make this world
a better place for himself, his fellow man, and his children.
But can he ever succeed? Are the improvements in human
society real improvements at all? Or are they all tainted with
sin and fallenness and accordingly hopeless and ultimately
useless?

The second society is that of the redeemed, the fellowship
of those who are in Christ, those who are partakers of divine
life, those who are new creations. Is this society then heaven
on earth? Does the church reveal the true nature of humanity
by its life, practices, and very existence? Theoretically, all
that is good must be found here. All that is honourable, just,
pure, lovely, gracious, of excellence, and worthy of praise
should be the basis of man in the redeemed society.

So there are two main questions. What *is* the difference
between man in these societies? What *should* the difference
be? All men are equally created, equally dust, equally fallen,
equally died for, equally created for glory. Or are they? Perhaps in the end we have to come back to *predestination.* Why
are some men members of only *one* society but not of both?
Why are some elect and not others? Should the elect any longer remain part of that first basic society or should they
separate themselves from man in his unredeemed society?

The answers to these questions are vital for our attitude
towards the possibility of social, legal, political and economic
change and the basis for such change. Can we recognize any
good thing outside the redeemed society? Will it last? Can we
work with agencies and philosophies which have a fundamentally different view of man and the world? Is there any
genuine hope for changing people in society? Is there any
means of changing society itself? Is the only means bringing
people into the community of the redeemed for that is where
true change happens?

These are questions to make us rethink our attitudes —
towards the world, in the sense of the non-Christian societies
in which we live and work, towards joint participation with
organizations and structures which are at base fundamentally
opposed to Christianity, and towards the nature of the
church and the redeemed community.

As a Baptist, I am intrigued by the middle ground which
churches like the Church of Scotland and the Church of England try to adopt. Here is a redeemed community which is yet
in theory fully integrated into a non-redeemed community.

The church is *established*. If the church can be truly and rightly totally integrated into a society and culture which have nothing much to say for or against Christianity (or are even opposed to it) and at the same time be the society of God's redeemed people, then that would solve the problem of the two societies. There would be no conflict. I confess to scepticism, and feel driven to hold some basic form of separation between the two societies and to uphold some fundamental differences between the members of one society and that of the other. To do anything else seems to entail the abandonment of the incarnational understanding of man through Christ.

I want now to turn attention to three problem areas in society and to say a word about the Christian approach to these problems. I shall deal with the theme of sex at greater length, but deal more briefly with race and individualism.

Individualism and Community

The classic evangelical position in the Protestant mould is personalistic. Jesus died for me. I receive Christ into my heart. Christ lives in me. I am on my way to heaven. Of course, I am delighted to find others who have Christ in their hearts too, but that simply reinforces my mission in life, to help each individual to a personal saving knowledge of Christ. The emphasis is on the person, on the individual, on each one deciding for himself or herself.

The so-called 'Social Gospel' was a stark reaction to all this. The gospel was about society, about changing society, about transforming communities, by changing conditions, structures, laws, setting, by creating new orders of life, new opportunities in life. If we created the right environment, then we would have shown the love of Christ, the gospel in action. Housing, education, leisure, culture — these were the key.

Neither of these extremes is as popular today, but we have a new approach to community. The Renewal Movement has brought many significant changes in its wake — the most relevant here is the charismatic community. The body picture of Corinthians is taken to a logical conclusion in the setting up of a charismatic household. Each member is part of the whole, the body; no part can exist or function properly without the rest. At the extreme this means that I do not

decide what I am going to do today, or this week, or with my
life or my future, or my career. The community decides. The
group of Spirit-filled Christians together will be led to God's
will for the community and thus each part of the community.
Personally I want to affirm the individual, to stress the personal responsibility, to uphold a strong notion of individuality but I see the crass extremes to which it leads.
Ultimately it is not simply individualistic, but existentialist, subjective and ultimately solipsistic. I inhabit my own
little world and there is no room for anything or anyone else.
So I must equally affirm that God makes individuals only
in the context of community. The extreme stress on community alone destroys individuality, and substitutes
totalitarian control for personal responsibility. Yet we are by
creation and nature social animals. For the Christian that
social basis is derived from God. It is not so much our common humanity, our shared culture, our similar race, or even
our nationhood (a Scot can say that); it is our creation in God.
So how then are we to be fully individuals in a right sense
but also fully social in a proper way? How may we bear our
own burden and also bear each other's burdens, without des-
troying each other's individuality yet fulfilling our social
natures? How can we learn from the charismatic stress on
community, without losing the truth of the Protestant stress
on the individual?

Sex.

Mankind comes in two packages, male and female. You cannot have one without the other, though all male clubs try and
some feminists would be equally glad to see one-sex rule.
None of us will deny that there is a real and crucial sense in
which women have needed to be liberated, though I imagine
that there might be a fairly hot debate as to whether the process has gone too far. If we are to say anything relevant about
man in society we cannot avoid talking about maleness and
femaleness. If we are hoping to present a true biblical anthropology we cannot pretend that Scripture has nothing to say
on the subject. Indeed the opposite is true. For many the
Bible has said too much and thus condemns itself. To understand man (in the generic sense) and to understand society we
must look at masculinity and feminity.
If we look closely at modern society we shall find that

stressing the role and the blatant oppression of women has led not to liberation for all, but to more subtle oppression, and to a corresponding demand for freedom from oppression for men, and, generally, more conflict between the sexes. Feminism, like chauvinism, polarizes the sexes from the start. Once the two have been torn asunder, no one can join them together. If there is to be any hope of men and women understanding who they are and the ways in which they can help each other grow, rather than thwart and stunt each other's development, it does not seem that the answer of feminism or reaction to feminism is without basic flaws.

There is an alternative.[9] The concept of maleness would have no meaning without the concept of femaleness and vice versa. If there were no women, not only would men soon cease to exist but there would be no significance at all to being a man. The only sense which would matter would be to differentiate man from animals and things. The first significant thing about humanity is not that it has two forms of sexuality, male and female. It is that people are different from animals and things. It is personhood, not sexuality, that is primary to people. Of course, persons happen to come in two particular packages, the female and the male person. But if there were a neuter person without specific sexual characteristics, we should still be faced with a person to be treated as human with all the rights and dignities of humanity. On the other hand, a male or female which was not a person, would be more like a vegetable or an animal. It would not be a member of the human race. Personhood is more basic than sexuality.

This will look like a side-stepping of the question 'What is a man?' and 'What is a woman?'. It is just that. It is not a refusal to examine male and female characteristics but a genuine attempt to shift the debate from a quicksand of sexual aggression and impasse, to an area where the initial unity of humanity and persons is realized. Sexual discrimination is not a problem about men or women, but about mankind both male and female. Two immediate questions face us. 'What is a person?' and 'What significance if any, does being a man or a woman have for a person?'.

What is a Person?

A person is made in the image of God. God makes a person

9. E. D. Cook, *Are Women People Too?* (Bramcote, Notts., 1978).

the person he or she is. Each person is created as a complex unity. Each has a body which enables him or her to feel. Each has a mind which seems to encapsulate the two aspects of thinking and willing. The person has a personality which can flower or be crushed, cope with situations or collapse in the light of them. To be a person is not the same as to be an animal or a thing. This seems to be bound up with consciousness, self-consciousness, and the ability to communicate. A person can be aware of himself or herself, has a sense of value and worth (or even of no value and worth), can choose to be self-centred or can try to develop in different directions.

To be a person is not just to have life. Quality of life matters. This is why cases of badly deformed children and accident victims who are like vegetables are hard. The loss of quality of life makes us uncertain as to their personal qualities. Are they persons at all? Treating people as persons is to assume their worth and their responsibility. We are not to walk all over people, because they are worth something — or were, or will be. They also have responsibility. That means that to be a person is to be answerable for what we do and say.

These aspects of humanity are primary to mankind. They form the basis for our relations with each other. Legal cases, cultural patterns, and social behaviour take root from these aspects of humanity. When it comes to regulating roles and to analysing at the most basic levels, it is the qualities which we call personal that matter most. Personhood ranks in importance before sexual identity. In our impersonal world the biggest threat to us all is of being reduced from a person to a thing or object. It is people who matter first and foremost rather than simply male people and female people.

What is Male and Female?

The male is physically stronger but less resilient, he is more independent, adventurous and aggressive, he is more ambitious and competitive, he has greater spatial, numerical and mechanical ability, he is more likely to construe the world in terms of objects, ideas and theories. The female at the outset possesses those sensory capacities which facilitate interpersonal communion; physically and psychologically she matures more rapidly, her verbal skills are precocious and proficient, she is more nurturant, affiliative, more consistent, and is likely to construe the world in personal, moral and aesthetic terms.[10]

10. C. Hutt, *Males and Females* (Harmondsworth, 1972), cited by Cook, *Are Women People Too?*, p. 9.

Even if this picture has only a grain of truth, it is one we are all familiar with. So where do the differences between men and women come from?

The first answer is biology. In terms of genetic structure, hormonal activity and basic physiology, women are different from men and always will be. Sexual differences are the products of nature. Ivor Mills, A. Storr and S. Goldberg have all argued that women cannot be more like men. To try to be so is to change nature which leads to unnatural consequences. On the other hand, feminists have argued equally cogently that women are women because of nurture, not nature. Social and cultural conditioning produces sex roles. The social, physical and psychological environment of western society makes little boys grow into men and girls into women. Patriarchy has produced what we call male and female characteristics. But if there were a matriarchal society things would be different. Feminists distinguish sexual (biological) identity from gender (cultural) identity. What matters most and what can be changed is gender identity. Different psychological and cultural approaches would produce different kinds of females and males. Men and women can exchange roles and functions. They need not conform to stereotype pictures. Women can be more like men and vice-versa. What is unique to one sex or the other is minimal and largely irrelevant. Different nurturing will produce different people.

Overcoming a natural tendency to say 'Vive la différence!', I must confess that it does not seem possible for the Christian, or anyone else, to give a categorical answer to the nature versus nurture question. One would need to be an expert geneticist, physiologist, biochemist, psychologist, sociologist and anthropologist all rolled into one and, more crucially, to be able to accept the presuppositions on which all these 'sciences' were based.

This does not mean the Christian has nothing to say about sexual/gender differences. God made the male and female. He made them as male and female. He created sexual differences. At this point it is clear that there is no superiority and no inferiority. There is basic difference. Difference to be explored, understood and accepted. Male and female have equal standing in the eyes of God. They are equally sinful. In Christ, they are equally redeemed. If that equality is worth anything, then both sexes have it. Both sexes need to explore their sexuality.

This is not the same as genitality. Masculine and feminine

seem to fall broadly into Hutt's classification, but that is not
to say that all sexual differences are fixed and that there are
no exceptions. People seem to cross any line drawn too rigid-
ly between the two sexes.

Society and culture have traditionally assigned certain roles
to women and others to men. We must ask, given sexual difference, what roles are appropriate for the sexes? Are some
totally inappropriate? To answer these questions we must examine the nature of the persons in the situations. What personal qualities are present? This is the primary way to assign
roles or question them. But this must happen not on paper,
but in real life, always remembering the reality of sexual difference.

Perhaps sexual differences are best understood not as a
blueprint to be forced on every specimen by rigid classification. Rather as a whole, they provide a map with some stable
points of reference, but also with uncharted areas in which we
may explore. Any explorer has to use what he/she knows in
order to explore what is not known. For the Christian such
exploration will happen in the context of the church using the
Bible as a guide-book.

Biblical Principles: Old Testament

The most important passage for understanding male and
female is Genesis 1-3. Not only is this the basis of the Old
Testament views but Jesus stresses it and Paul uses it as the
foundation of his theological argument. The basic qualities
of personhood stem from God and his creation of persons.
Then we read that God made two kinds of people in his
image. Men and women are made to complement each other.
Woman is to be a helper to man. The man is to take responsibility for woman, as he does in naming her. That was
the creation ideal, but both fall from God's standard and that
means broken relationships with God and with each other.
All too easily we fall from partnership before God into positions of domineering and cowering. That is true for all
women and men, not just married folk. The only solution is
to replace misleading talk of equality by complementarity,
that is, each other fulfilling the best for the other before God.

One link between the Old and New Testaments is the idea
of headship. In 1 Cor. 12-14 we must note that all are under
headship. This is not something anti-women. It affects men

as much as women. God is the head of all. Christ is the head of man and man of woman. This headship is not some male plot to keep pushy women in their place, for it comes from God. Men have a place as much as women and both are to keep to their proper roles. This is why the behaviour of both men and women is at stake in Paul's mind, not just that of women. If a woman wishes to reject the idea of headship, she is not so much rebelling against man, as against God. Headship implies that man is responsible for woman; it is interesting that God comes to Adam first though it is Eve who has sinned first. The idea of man as head is cold comfort for the male chauvinist. Inasmuch as that sets demands for women, it equally sets demands for men to behave and act towards women in proper ways. All too often men's behaviour towards women is not so much headship, but self-centred domineering. This is why Paul exhorts husbands to love their wives as Christ loved the church and sacrificed himself for her (Eph. 5:25). The headship of man in relation to women is never an end in itself, but is always under Christ's headship of man, and God's of Christ. Barth sums up the point in a helpful way: 'The essential point is that woman must always and in all circumstances be woman; that she must feel and conduct herself as such and not as a man; that the command of the Lord, which is for all eternity, directs both man and woman to their own proper sacred place and forbids all attempts to violate this order.'[11] No idea of subordination — being of a different order — can be demanded without leading to fatal legalism. Christ offered obedience to God in love. Man cannot demand obedience, but woman, in love, can offer a right response to man. The law kills, but the Spirit gives life. There is an aim in subordination. It is to fulfil both sexes properly in being what God intended. Woman was made for man not by man himself, but by the Lord. This is why both are totally mutually dependent. Their very life depends on each other and likewise does the fulfilment of God's purpose for mankind.

Paul is clearly teaching that a different place in the order of creation does not contradict mutual dependence. Rather it enhances it. The point in any subordination is not for one sex to glory over another, but that the partnership might be more fruitful and more lovely for both and so for God. In the end, man and woman together are answerable for what they make of the world God gives them. Such accountability naturally

11. Karl Barth, *Church Dogmatics*, vol. III: 4 (Edinburgh, 1961), p. 156.

may mean different kinds of responsibilities, but these are not independent from each other nor inferior or superior to each other.

For many, talk of subordination or subjection is too much to stomach. It would be if this was one sex foisting its views on the other. But all of creation is in subjection to something or someone. To pretend otherwise is to reject all authority over us and to imagine that each individual can do exactly as he or she likes and be his or her own boss. A more accurate description of the basic nature of sin would be hard to find.

New Testament

Galatians 3:28 seems to proclaim the full effect of Christ's victory over the fall. In Christ the basic distinctions which can separate people are overcome. Our problem is to make that reality come to pass initially in the church and eventually in the world. Theologically, redemption by Christ and the indwelling of the Spirit are the heart of the New Testament. Men and women are equally redeemed and indwelt. Christ and the Spirit do not obliterate a person, but allow the full growth and development of manhood and womanhood. Our task is to help each other, all too conscious that the effects of the fall are being overcome, but that the final overcoming will only be seen at the end. So we live in the tension between Christ's complete victory and its future complete realization. The example of women and men's relationships with them from Christ to Paul reflects that tension. Even in the presence of Christ, women, like men, do the wrong thing. Martha gets it wrong, while Mary gets it right.

We are not to belittle each other, but to build each other up. What is true for the church as a whole is true for individual men and women, whether married or not. In the perfect re-creation in Christ, this is now truly possible by the Spirit who dwells in us.

Concluding Postscript on Sex

The feminist debate has drawn attention to the breakdown of right relationships between men and women. How are Christians to respond? First, we need to be careful about accepting suggested prescriptions, for the very diagnosis of the disease may rest on anti-Christian views. We need to take the problem seriously but to refocus the debate towards the question how all people should relate properly as persons, and then apply this to male-female relationships.

Perhaps modern society talks too much about male and female, but does little to explore the depths of man-woman relationships. As with the seed of the gospel, the work of change is slow. Society will only begin to change, to question its own views and practices, when it recognizes the failure of its present attempts and the possibility of different ones. The debasement of both sexes is obvious in the way they treat each other. There is hope for change if a new pattern of man-and-woman relationships can be discovered.

The redeemed community of the church is the best place to reveal God's pattern of man-and-woman relationships. This means that church practices and male-female relationships need to be closely examined. In what ways are we following cultural patterns? In so doing, are we allowing the world to mould us? In what ways are biblical principles in fact being worked out? All traditions must be brought to the bar of the Bible.

It is clear in Scripture that men and women are meant to be different to complement each other and so complete God's perfect plan for the world. How can we order the church so that this mutual support is fostered? Without a proper balancing of the sexes, the result will be less than the best. Headship and subordination are relevant not only to women but to men also. Both are under authority and bear responsibility before God. This inevitably means that women were not made to do all that man does, or vice versa, but if the one fails to do his or her job properly, then the other may take his or her place. There are limits to the exchanging of roles. Men cannot be women and sexual differences must remain.

So let us explore masculinity and femininity within the loving context of the church, where we can afford to make mistakes recognizing that God's grace is always sufficient. Let us use the Bible as the test for practices and attitudes to each other. Let us learn to complement each other properly. As always the real solution lies in the example of Jesus, the servant. It means an all-round change of heart with both sexes renouncing bossing and bossiness but each reckoning the other better than oneself, taking responsibility for each other and facilitating the growth and development of each other and the exercising of gifts and graces by both. In all this we are co-workers with God, for the man-woman relationship relies not on men and women, but on God.

Race

A recent *Observer* article bemoaned the genuine difficulty a brilliant black teacher had in trying to get to the top in an education system which was white and racist. The cry was clear: how many black teachers are there in schools which are predominantly West Indian, or Asian teachers where the kids are Asian?

Here is the racist vicious circle. You have a racist white system. In seeing the wrong in it, you create — not an integrated system — but a racist black system. The whites teach the whites and the blacks the blacks. Muhammed Ali summed it up, 'Like mates with like — you don't find butterflies mating with birds; so keep to your own and we'll keep to ours'.

We could spend hours examining the racial problem, in terms of conditions and attitudes, and the cures suggested, but at the very heart of it all for me lies the attraction of like and the fear of unlike.

I have time for two comments. The first is that we shall never understand the race problem, far less go any way to solving it, until we all admit that we are racists. We are all prejudiced. If our social and civil legislation began at that point, then the laws and our understanding of racial problems might be very different.

This leads directly to the second comment. The ideal at present is integration. Yet by making special categories and special procedures, we are in danger of reinforcing and institutionalizing the very differences and prejudices that the special efforts are designed to obliterate. Do we really want integration? Does anybody want it? What will it really mean? If society is to be a cohesive unit, how much difference can we take, and how much similarity does there need to be? Baldwin's question to the American Negro is highly relevant to the Black Rhodesian, South African and indeed British West Indian or Asian, 'Do I want to be *integrated* into a burning house?' What price integration?

At the outset I stressed the need to be clear about our biblical anthropology before we embarked on the application to society. But inevitably it is meeting with and coming to terms with the plurality of cultures in our society which will sharpen our understanding of man, and enable us to apply biblical insights to our social, legal, economic, political, and theological functioning. The areas where the need for clarification is most urgent are: individualism and collectivism; sex; race. But I think there are clues which will help us in these areas and in understanding man in society in general.

The first is the reaching of a proper balance between me, us and them. What am I, and what is proper for me, as an individual to do and be? Who are we? What makes us a community? How do we, how should we function as a community? If our community includes, it also excludes. Who are left out? How are we to think of them? What separates us from them and should it?

For me the second clue lies in the understanding that to be human is to be responsible and answerable. If we are concerned to be fully human, we must learn to take and shoulder proper responsibility. If we are concerned to help others to become more human, we must help them take responsibility, yet without shelving our own responsibility for and to them. We are to bear each other's burdens, as well as bear our own burdens.

The third clue lies in the nature of *koinonia* — fellowship. What kind of social cohesion is fellowship? Is it unique, or is the pub as much a fellowship as the church meeting? How much pluralism can the fellowship of the church stand? Do we need to bring a test of orthodoxy and heresy?

The fourth clue I do not pretend to understand, but I am sure it is vital for man and society. It is creativity. Behind this lies the creativity of God, which man made in his image must learn to express properly. I use the term 'art', but 'science' or a great many other things would do equally well. I take this to mean various things, for example, art for art's sake. It is an expression or extension of me and my personality or me and my group's ideas. For the purist it means art for its own sake. It is just there, it does not carry a message, it does not state. It is simply there because it has its own value regardless of what I, the artist, think it is, or how you, the observers, react to it. Then there is the kind of creativity which we tend to belittle by calling it applied or technological art for society's sake. We feel there is something less than pure and artistic about pragmatic art. Yet why should creativity be useless rather than useful?

In the church and in society at large, we need to encourage and express creativity in all these sense. This will be part of our fulfilment as men and women in society.

Reading List

G. C. Berkouwer, *Man: the Image of God* (London, 1972).

E. Brunner, *Man in Revolt* (London, 1939).

G. Carey, *I Believe in Man* (London, 1978).

J. Moltmann, *Man: Christian Anthropology in the Conflicts of the Present* (London, 1974).

R. Niebuhr, *The Nature and Destiny of Man*, 2 vols. (London, 1941-43).

D. Williams, *About People* (Leicester, 1978).

Questions for Discussion

1   Is there really any difference between man in the society of the church and man in society at large? What are the differences? What should they be?

2   Must we choose between 'me' and 'us'? What is the right relation between the two?

3   What is the relevance to measures designed to counter racism of (a) the fall, and (b) redemption in Christ?

4   Is what really matters in the end being human or being Christian? If we say 'Christian' have we denied our humanity, and humanity's humanity?

5   How far do the elements of a Christian social anthropology presented in this chapter provide guidance in tackling social issues such as education, punishment of offenders, unemployment?

Chapter Seven
Human Rights
John Gladwin

CHAPTER SEVEN

Human Rights

The Evangelical Dilemma

I BELIEVE WE ARE HUNG UP ON 'RIGHTS'. PLEASE DON'T misunderstand. I am all for human rights, for equality, for the right of every person to make his or her unique contribution to the world. My fear is that, in our struggle for rights, we have gone so far that we are in danger of forgetting how redemptive the voluntary laying aside of certain 'rights' can be. It's possible that the demand for our rights can become a self-centred way of life.[1]

There we have expressed, in somewhat emotive language, the dilemma of evangelical Christianity when facing the human rights movement. On the one hand, we do not want to be found upholding tyranny and oppression in either its crude or its subtle forms in society. On the other hand, talk of and campaigning for human rights seems to betray something at the heart of the gospel. 'He who does not take his cross and follow me is not worthy of me. He who finds his life will lose it, and he who loses his life for my sake will find it' (Matt. 10: 38-39).

At one level, one can have a lot of sympathy with much evangelical reticence in getting involved and committed in the socio-political cauldron of the modern world. So much that is

---

1. Ann Smith, in *Vital Christianity* 15.1.1978.

going on takes place in a context of alien thinking marked by
conflict which all too often breaks out in actual violence, with
tyranny replacing tyranny, and little apparent common
ground to appeal to for socio-political conduct.

Yet I believe that the gospel leaves us no choice. If it is
about the saving word of God coming to us in the midst of
history and change, and if it concerns the saving of human
life through the self-offering and life of the man Christ Jesus,
then it sets its children unavoidably in compassionate concern
for human life, in all its turmoil, in the heart of the history of
the world. Today it is impossible to consider our response to
our neighbour outside of the social context which shapes him
and which in turn he shapes. I cannot avoid standing next to
another who, for whatever reason, struggles on behalf of the
victims of the world, seeking to protect the weak and the
poor from the strong and to establish their human rights in
the face of the endeavours of power to exclude them for fac-
tional and short-term interest. It is God who chooses the
weak and the foolish to confound the strong and the wise.
This has been the mark of his saving work from its outset in
our history.

Moreover, at the level of the shaping of the human mind
and in the ongoing process of developing and reforming
norms of social activity, the contemporary concern for
human rights leads us on to consider our own understanding
of the nature and purpose of human life, the duties and
powers of political institutions, and the relationship of freedom and justice, and always in the context of our commitment to Jesus Christ. Great biblical themes are touched upon
in this issue.

It is with this latter level — the shaping of our minds —
that we are primarily concerned in this conference, not in
detachment from the daily pressures of politics, human suffering and pain, but in our fundamental commitment and concern to influence and develop a praxis in conformity to the
gospel as witnessed to in Holy Scripture. We want God's
word to become a living and blazing fire in our bones which
cannot be contained but bursts out of our beings in action for
our neighbour.

Enlightenment Beginnings

Where, however, are we to begin in considering the development of the human rights movement and its root principles? My choice of the Enlightenment may seem an arbitrary one. We must begin somewhere remembering that our choice of starting point is itself set in a context of history. However, I do believe that the changing philosophical themes of the Enlightenment, in the context of the political developments of the eighteenth century, marked such a step forward in our western society that thought and experience, human expectations and norms of conduct, were shifted in a new direction. Empiricism, a love of reason, a search for the natural order, and a philosophical and political concern for the 'inalienable rights of man' come to life in the eighteenth-century context. Such thinking and struggle takes on political reality in the shape of the American Constitution, in the declarations of the French Revolution, and in the writings of Tom Paine. From Locke at the end of the seventeenth century to Rousseau in the eighteenth century we encompass a range of developing thought about the nature of politics and the relationship of the individual to the political community which has left a lasting imprint upon the mind of subsequent generations.

Evangelical Antecedents

Before we comment upon this tradition and where it leads us today, it is worth noting that we, as Evangelicals, are not without forebears in this business of concern for the rights of people as citizens and members of human society. It may be that part of our trouble is that we are children of another eighteenth-century reality, the evangelical awakening, which stood in opposition to the rationalism of its times and was derided as 'enthusiasm', which Bishop Butler called 'a very horrid thing'.[2] Although that revival did lead into practical and compassionate activity in society, such as the movement to abolish the slave trade, the work of the Clapham Sect, and later on the work of Shaftesbury and others, it never produced a rounded theology of church and society. For this reason, at least in part, piety and reason, religion and politics, have been set in tension with each other in the evangelical tradition.

Yet, we have a larger inheritance than that represented in

2. See G. R. Cragg, *The Church and the Age of Reason, 1648-1789* (Harmondsworth, 1970), p. 150.

the eighteenth- and nineteenth-century awakenings. There are other places in history from which we take sustenance. The Reformation, for example, as one such place in the Christian past, did seek a concept of social order. It struggled deeply with the meaning of its developing theology for the state and for the activity of government. It sought to come to terms with the extent and the limits of political power and with the duties and rights of citizens and of the officers of the law in the face of tyranny.[3] Even if in our retrospective judgement both Luther and Calvin failed to drive home the full significance of their understanding of freedom in Christ alone for the political order, the shape of a theology appropriate to the issues is still present in their work.

It was not only mainstream Protestant history and thinking, but also the Anabaptist tradition which contributed to the development of our freedoms. As Alan Kreider has shown, in a paper given at the Westminster Conference in 1975, the Baptists had a clear understanding of the extent and limits of state power. Their name has been spoilt by some of the wild and extreme social and religious experimentation on the fringes of the movement.[4]

In our own country we owe more than is sometimes admitted to the Puritan tradition and its struggle in the seventeenth century. The commitment of our state institutions to the rule of law and to the subjection of government to the rule of law owes much to the Puritans' refusal to yield absolute authority to any but God himself. It was they who took on the brunt of the struggle against the Stuart idea of the divine right of kings.

So, if this subject appears to be a strange one for modern evangelical ears, it is not because it lacks precedent in the past but rather because of our neglect in our more recent experience. Thankfully, in this highly political age, there are signs that the movement is looking to rectify these more recent omissions so that we in our turn can make our contribution to the development of a proper biblical understanding of politics, of the state, and of citizenship.

Locke and Social Contract

In considering the central issue at stake in the human rights

3. John Calvin, *Institutes of Christian Religion* IV:20:31-32.
4. Alan Kreider, 'The Anabaptists', in *The Christian and the State in Revolutionary Times* (London, 1975), pp. 28ff.

movement we must consider the development of the philosophy and politics of rights in the period of the Enlightenment. In a wholly prejudiced comment on Rousseau, given
under the cover of academic objectivity, Bertrand Russell sets
the scene for us:

> Ever since his time, those who considered themselves reformers
> have been divided into two groups, those who followed him
> (Rousseau) and those who followed Locke. Sometimes they co-
> operated, and many individuals saw no incompatibility. But
> gradually the incompatibility has become increasingly evident.
> At the present time, Hitler is the outcome of Rousseau; Roose-
> velt and Churchill, of Locke.[5]

In itself, Russell's statement is an insolence to Rousseau and
excessively charitable to both Roosevelt and Churchill. Yet,
in a perverse sort of way, it highlights the key issue for us
over human rights and the problem associated with them.

In his exposition of Locke, Russell points out that the
social contract idea is hinted at in Aquinas, clearly explicated
in Grotius, and given a particular form in Locke. We may
note in them all a common concern to discover the natural
law or the natural order. There is a given order of things, laws
which define the proper boundaries of what ought or ought
not to pertain. It is this natural order, and its partner, the
natural and inalienable rights of men, which are at the
foundation of the creation of civil society. According to
Locke, society is founded not upon some direct link between
divine authority and the institutions of government but upon
the voluntary yielding to the community of individual rights
for the protection of life and property. Therefore, rather than
having an absolute authority to do as it pleases, government
has a power and responsibility which derive from their origin
in the inalienable rights of individuals over life and property.
In his Hamlyn Lectures entitled *Liberty, Law and Justice* Sir
Norman Anderson says, 'It is not always realized that it was
the doctrine of Natural Law which was the direct progenitor
of the concept of Human Rights'.[6] He maintains that rationalism turned a concept of natural law, founded upon the
divine order, into one of natural rights which stands in its
own autonomy on the foundation of human reason.

For Locke, the social contract is something which people
make as a way of protecting their natural rights in society. So

5. Bertrand Russell, *History of Western Philosophy* (London, 1946), p. 660.
6. J. N. D. Anderson, *Liberty, Law and Justice* (London, 1978), pp. 19ff.

the protection of individual rights is the purpose of the social contract and consent is its means. In a formative work entitled *A Theory of Justice* John Rawls has sought to revive the social contract theory for our own time.[7] He is concerned to provide a firmer foundation for the survival of liberal democracy than is provided in the predominant utilitarianism of our century. Rawls asks what a group of rational people, thinking about the basis of society without knowing how history would treat them or others in society, would agree to concerning the normative principles on which such a society would function. By insisting that such a group work from a position of ignorance about the eventual outcome, Rawls has sought to remove all that might prejudice sound rational judgement. Such a group of people, claims Rawls, would arrive at a social contract which they would accept as binding whatever the outcome. That social contract would have two foundation principles. Its basic commitment would be to freedom. Equal liberty would be a fundamental principle. The second principle after liberty would be that of justice — an agreement to economic and social sharing. Liberty is basic but it needs justice as its partner to guarantee a fair and reasonable society. Whenever society was faced with a demand which infringed these principles its basic commitment to the contract would enable it to draw back. Political and legal institutions would enshrine the principles of the contract. The right to liberty and to justice would be guaranteed by contract.

There is a strong tendency in the social contract tradition to see man in the social context as a bundle of rights which it is the duty of society to safeguard. In the eighteenth-century debate this was seen as basic to the natural order of things and therefore basic to proper political reasoning. This can be seen in the Declaration of Independence in the United States of America, where it is asserted as self-evident 'that all men are created equal and that they are endowed by their Creator with certain inalienable rights', including life and liberty and the pursuit of happiness. In the declaration of the French National Assembly in 1789 it was 'resolved to lay down in a solemn Declaration, the natural, inalienable and sacred Rights of Man'.

This has set the context for political thinking and action over human rights ever since. The experience of tyranny and

---

7. John Rawls, *A Theory of Justice* (Cambridge, Mass., 1971).

oppression in our own century have increased public concern for human rights throughout the world. The experience of the holocaust in Nazi Germany and of the Second World War led to the creation of the United Nations and to its own Declaration of Human Rights in 1948. All member states are committed to this declaration. The continued experience of genocide and mass political extermination, of the gross abuse of political power in torture and oppression all over the modern world, has added to the sense of urgency in many quarters to see governments practise a commitment to the U.N. Declaration. Since 1948 the concern for rights has spread beyond that of political rights *vis-à-vis* the state, to economic and social rights of a very diverse kind. Sir Norman Anderson's Hamlyn Lectures detail the flood of declarations and statements on rights which cover economic, cultural, legal, political, social and sexual matters.[8] So what was once a classic small list of essential rights — life, liberty, happiness, property — has become a great bundle of rights. We now talk about children's rights, women's rights, gay rights, animal rights, and so on across a wide field of concern.

If Christians have difficulty assenting to the confidence of the eighteenth-century rationalists in the capacity of reason to discover from the natural order universally agreed foundations for the social defence of universally justifiable rights of men, how much more are we going to have trouble providing a secure basis for our modern extension of the list of rights? If there is a danger within the social contract and rights tradition from Grotius onwards of considering it possible to provide justification for society without any reference to the creator, Christians are going to be very wary of any tendency in modern thought to close political order in on itself and leave it no defence against those who, for a variety of reasons, will not uphold what others consider to be reasonable and right.

In this sense Sir Norman's concern to secure natural law inside a creation order is a proper concern to drive us to think about the nature and work of God undergirding social order. This way of thinking about human activity in society — of viewing people in society in terms of rights and set in contractual relationships to each other and to government — contains the danger of undermining neighbourly love in community. In Locke, the prime reason for having society is for

8. *Op. cit.* pp. 40f.

the defence of certain basic rights. The defence of my neighbour's rights is effectively a way of protecting my own. Thus there is a strong individualism running through this tradition in the human rights/social contract idea. Society is seen here as a careful balance in which I pass over to the state the responsibility to defend my life and property for the sake of peace and order. The strong individualism of the autonomous man in such thinking has contributed to the development of political democracy and limits to state power. However, in its inherent selfishness over rights it runs the risk of cutting the individual off from being bound to his neighbour in a bond of free and unselfish service.

Rousseau and Collectivism

As Bertrand Russell has suggested, Rousseau represents a wholly different type of tradition. There can be no doubt about his influence on the modern world. Rousseau tried to resolve the problems of the individual and society and of freedom and justice. He has had a very bad press in many quarters of which Russell would be a good example. Interestingly enough, one of the most sympathetic and penetrating analyses of his work *Du Contract Social* is the one by Karl Barth in *Protestant Theology in the Nineteenth Century*. Rousseau understood society to be a matter of secondary order. The natural order has been lost to us. In the natural order human life was marked by pure individual freedom. Society, as we know it, was created by man through the acquisition of property. 'The first man who, having enclosed a piece of land, bethought himself of saying "This is mine" and found enough to believe him was the real founder of civil society.'[9]

Rousseau was concerned that this secondary creation of civil society should be marked by the justice which was present in the original natural order (now lost). This is how Barth understands Rousseau:

> The problem of the state is rather how to bring about a union between men which by its corporate might shields every individual in such a manner that he is at once one with the whole and yet free, and free — i.e. obeying himself alone — by virtue of this very consent. The basic act which represents the answer

9. Cited from *Oeuvres de J. J. Rousseau* (Amsterdam, 1769), vol. 2, by Karl Barth, *Protestant Theology in the Nineteenth Century* (London, 1972), p. 188.

to this problem is an act of submission, the complete transference by the individual of all his rights to the community as such. It is precisely by everyone giving himself completely — not to somebody but to all, and not all as the sum of every individual, but to all as the public person which has arisen out of their union.[10]

So Rousseau introduced the concept of the sovereignty of the people, not as a company of individuals but as the public person to which all have yielded their rights voluntarily — not to the state as government within society, but the whole people together. Rousseau added to this the idea that the general will of the people could be expressed through the majority. Rousseau does not say that the state gives rights, but that in the social contract the individual has yielded his rights and exercises them henceforth only through the collective will of the people who together form the public person. In this way Rousseau and collectivism have a great deal in common. It does not surprise us, therefore, to find political thinkers like Mao to be students of Rousseau.

If the problem of liberal democracy, in the tradition of Locke, is the threat of a selfish individualism to the well-being of the community, the problem of collectivism is its constant threat to the integrity of the individual. In practice this type of theory easily degenerates into state manipulation of individuals into the given ideal pattern for social order.

Thus in collectivist states the problem for human rights is the constant attack on individuals who do not voluntarily conform to the social theory the creation of the state. In Marxist countries, where in theory there ought to be a movement towards the perfect order in which government and state disappear, politics gets stuck in practice at the point of the maximum state commitment to the moulding of the whole life of the community into a specific social pattern. Thus the individual conscience is threatened, in collectivism, by the heteronomous state.

Tension Between Freedom and Justice

At the heart of this matter is the classic problem of the relationship of freedom and justice. If we say that man (and I use the term in its generic sense to cover both male and female

10. *Ibid.*

persons equally) possesses inalienable rights and then try to define them (e.g. the U.N. Declaration 1948, the European Convention 1950), what happens when these rights seem to be in conflict with each other? The practical deployment of rights involves others in the community. Consider the abortion debate as an example. If, as some say, the woman is to have the final say over the fate of the foetus because it is her body and she is carrying the child so that it is an affront to her autonomy for others to have a decisive voice in the matter, how is this position to be matched with the close involvement of others in the problem? Does not the unborn child have rights, and does not the father have rights? If one group are saying 'the woman's rights' and another 'the child's rights' and yet a third 'the father's rights', how is the clash to be resolved except through struggle and the law trying to act as an umpire in the middle? This way of understanding the matter is implicitly destructive of mutual love and service, in this case in the small community of the family.

Let us consider a wider social issue, rights in education. We may talk of 'parents' rights' and provide an element of choice within an education system to preserve the rights of parents. Yet children have rights as well; how are these to be protected against the abuse of parental rights? What if, in a desire to preserve the rights of parents, the rights of children are severely limited? As one headmaster of a comprehensive school said to me recently, 'Parental choice means a perpetuation of advantage for already advantaged groups of children'. Are human rights and freedoms now in fundamental conflict with the claims of justice?

It is problems like these which drive the state to collectivist solutions. Yet, if it is a collectivist type of social contract, what is to happen to those citizens who wish to live quiet and peaceful lives and yet for reasons of conscience cannot conform to every aspect of the collective ideal? The problems of minority groups in the state are age-old. Minority race groups like the Jews, the sects, and other minority religious groups, are continually under pressure in strong states committed to definitive ideologies of politics.

The highlighting of these problems in human rights thinking from the Enlightenment on is not aimed at detaching Christians from a commitment to many of the issues at stake in the modern human rights movement. Indeed, it is important to say that the silent inactivity of Christians in the face of tyranny and oppression is a sin against God in its failure to act for one's neighbour in his time of need. What we are concerned about is the shape of mind which lies at the roots of the movement. Practical trouble is bound to persist if inadequate thinking underlies the action. In particular, that sort of thinking which appears to suggest that individuals possess 'rights' to be given or kept in relation to the community or that the state can withhold or bestow these rights, seems bound to lead to a conflict between freedom and justice to be resolved only in a delicate and uneasy contract in civil society.

In making these criticisms one cannot but be aware of the lack of a serious evangelical contribution to this vital social question. If, in looking at the buildings which others have created to provide a defence against tyranny, we can see some weaknesses, some cracks, some badly guarded points, we have to confess that we have still to attend to laying foundations, let alone putting up a structure which will survive the insidious attacks of the oppressors. Our task must have humility as its virtue and modesty in its claims.

Christian Contribution to the Human Rights Issue

The biblical witness leaves us no choice but compassionate identification in the struggle for justice for the many who suffer through their powerlessness at the hands of tyrants and oppressors. This commitment shares, in its own way, in the search for a more human politics. The knowledge of God and compassionate involvement cannot be torn asunder in Christian thought and practice. It is the gospel which provides us with the clues to a way forward.

A good deal of the theological ground-work for this subject is dependent on the contributions *Man in Society* and *Towards a Theology of the State* contained elsewhere in this volume. I cannot avoid touching briefly on three themes to do with our understanding of man.

1. *Man is created* in the image and likeness of God. We believe that what man is and possesses is a consequence of the graciousness of God our creator. Life has its origin and its purpose in God and depends upon him for its continuance and well-being. It is through creation and because of the covenant God has made with man that man enjoys the place which he does in the world with his neighbours. This continues to be the case, even in a fallen and corrupt world, by the grace of God. After the flood, God made a covenant with

Noah promising to bless him and his descendants and never again to destroy the earth by flood. Underneath our life together in the world are the grace and concern of God our creator. What we are has its origin not within ourselves nor in human society but in God. So we are bound to be cautious about talk of rights as though they are a personal and individualistic possession or as though they are within the gift of the state or the community at large. The autonomy of the individual or the heteronomy of the community implicit in the anthropocentric approach of the humanist tradition cannot adequately bear the full weight of the Christian understanding of man who has his freedom and his life as a gift and stewardship from God.

2. What man possesses from God as a free gift is to be used in ways which reflect the graciousness of the Giver. In our outgoing relationships in family and society we are to deploy the good gifts of God within the pattern learnt from God's own generosity to us. So the grace of God sets its own limits and boundaries to human conduct and to the use of such gifts as power in society. Just as Christian freedom and license do not go together neither do *responsible stewardship* and absolutism in society. It is God who teaches me that I am to exercise the power and gifts over which I have control not so much in pursuit of my freedom and happiness (with the restriction that this must not be at others' expense, as in John Rawls' idea) as creatively for others in support of their human well-being.

3. Christians locate the problem of the individual in conflict with society and its claims in the effects of *our human fallenness*. It is our loss of the knowledge and love of God which has destroyed creative community and shut in the individual behind a wall of shame, making him afraid of the world and of commitment to others. It is this fearful individual when brought into society who continually runs the risk of exploiting what power comes his way in self-defence against others who appear to threaten him as he does them.

The Gospel and Human Rights

Man as creature, man as responsible steward, and man as fallen are an integral part of the Christian faith as it approaches the dilemma over human rights. Let us consider man, in addition to this, in the light of the central theme of our Christian faith — the gospel. It is after all the gospel of the free unmerited grace of God to sinners in Jesus Christ, received through faith, which is at the heart of our evangelical experience. At the centre of this is the gracious work of God for us in the self-giving of Jesus Christ to the extremity of death on the cross for the sin of mankind. The key to the new life in the world of God's kingdom is to be found in Jesus Christ crucified and risen. What can we learn about human rights from the man from heaven?

1. We learn of *one who, perfectly established in his Father's freedom and will, spared no cost in meeting the needs of others.* Tempted to assert his power and status for self-interest and glory, he set his face in another direction in which he was called to give without limit in compassionate response to the needs of others. Here is a way of love which achieves something for the world as well as setting it an example in human life of the character of love itself. Christ's love is actually creative in achieving its purpose and thereby creating a new community called to witness to the kingdom of God. In Christ freedom, experienced in the knowledge and love of God, leads to service through self-giving without limit for the sake of a broken and fallen world.

The God who is the giver of life, who is its source and sustenance, and who alone has an ultimate right over life, is the one who in his Son gives life for the freedom of a fallen and enslaved humanity.

It is the love of God manifest in Jesus Christ which reveals the eternal value which God places upon human life and which the world abuses, spoiling the gifts he gives it. Here we see a holy identification with man in his wretchedness and weakness. This is the love which responds in freedom and compassion to the victims of the world — the poor, the sick, the rejected, and the powerless. Those, therefore, who look for their own lives to grow into the image of the life of the man from heaven are called to validate their commitment through this heavenly love shaping their human relationships and concerns. The struggle with and for the victims of power abuse in the world in the practical outworking of compassion is central to obedience to the love of God.

We must not run away from the practical demands for action because it will mean sharing concerns with others who may not share our convictions. Even though the humanist building has weaknesses in its structure, if its practical concerns fall within the boundaries of the demands of compassion and justice in the light of the gospel we must share them in the political arena. A theology for politics which is necessarily detached and implicitly perfectionist cannot hope to cope with the practical demands for present action. The problems for Christian action of this sort can be illustrated from a conversation which I had with a member of the anti-Nazi League.

This young Christian was concerned both by the domination of that organization by the Socialist Workers Party and by the almost total lack of support for him and other concerned Christians from the church in the struggle against the bully boys who scapegoat the ethnic minority groups for the ills of our society. He was concerned at the risks of his commitment and the loneliness of his chosen path in the Christian fellowship.

2. The gospel teaches us that *the act of yielding rights and power in the cause of justice is creative for human life and possibilities.* It is not those who stand on their rights who achieve the truly human goals. Those who run the risks, refuse to stand by their position and their life and are ready to try new things irrespective of the possible cost to self — they are the ones who through compassion open up hope in social activity. 'Let this mind be in you which was in Jesus Christ, who being in the form of God thought it not robbery to be equal with God; but made himself of no reputation, and took upon himself the form of a servant, and was made in the likeness of men' (Phil. 2:5ff.).

Christ achieves our salvation through action in which power and status are yielded for others, and thereby calls a new humanity into being. There are many situations today where the conflict is between power grimly held on to and rights demanded and fought for through struggle. Southern Africa offers an obvious example. If only those who possess the power and the rights knew the way of freedom in risking their position for the possibility of a new community founded on justice! The determination of power that it shall not fall into other hands forces those on the receiving end of its abuses into deeper and deeper conflict and struggle. Here the risks are that the community will be so badly fractured in the struggle that factionalism and strife will continue to mark the life of society into the distant future. The abuses of power lead to communities asserting their own human dignity through the discovery of the integrity of their own separate life and culture — black consciousness, red consciousness, women's consciousness. The danger is always present, however, that such 'consciousness' will attempt to fossilize itself at the point of division and so lose the possibility of a common fellowship of black and white, male and female, Protestant and Catholic, Jew and Arab beyond the stereotyped ghetto politics of struggle. If the struggle against oppression offers the possibility of a new beginning for society it always runs the risk of collapsing beyond victory into a new oppression. The legitimate Christian presence in the struggle for the removal of the indignities imposed upon many groups in our world by the powerful must be a presence which seeks to humanize power and the struggle for it, by means of the Christian story of the one who was both willing and able to yield self creatively for others.

3. The third truth which becomes apparent in the gospel is *the fundamental respect which we ought to have for the integrity of the consciences of other people.* The way of Jesus Christ, of self-emptying, of yielding rights, is a way which meets others with freedom in forgiveness. Christ does not barge through the protective wall of our conscience and our shame. The gospel does not involve a rape of the individual person. Indeed the gospel presents us with Jesus Christ as the one who alone has the right to approach the inner self because he comes to justify rather than condemn, to forgive rather than to judge. Because of his unique work in redemption, because he has known our human predicament, even to the point of the cross, he comes to us as a brother affirming our dignity. Because he approaches us as the one who alone can still our troubled and guilty consciences he can approach the inner sanctuary of our heart. Because he approaches with the free gift of love and does not come as an oppressor to make impossible demands of us he alone can turn us from the fearful self-protection which marks our living towards a new way of service in love and so to growth to maturity in human life.

Such a gospel points us to a new way in which the fundamental freedom and integrity of the person becomes the foundation for true fellowship in service through Christ. When we have been met by Jesus Christ bringing us good news we can no longer treat others in ways which infringe their dignity and sanctity of life. The basic integrity of another cannot be raped by any form of social or personal manipulation by any one whose life has found freedom in forgiveness through Jesus Christ. The individualism of the gospel leads towards community. It leads towards a community in which differences in human life and personal experience do not become, as in a fallen world, a cause for the breakdown of community, but the seed-bed of a fellowship which emphasises both the *common* humanity of all and the importance of *diversity* within the whole.

Human relationships in the church which are patterned on Christ's love for us witness in the world to a way in which human dignity and community are established in service to others. In the midst of the world's struggle to guard human rights and dignity the Christian testimony to Jesus Christ 'salts' the wider concern for rights. The Christian presence is vital in this aspect of our life in the world.

4. If true freedom is established by the grace of God and my life is made forfeit at the cross and restored to me as a gift in the service of the kingdom of God, then *my participation in the politics of the present time does not have to be inhibited by fear of what will happen to self.* Neither intimidation from outside nor the paralysis of fear within need prevent me taking needed action in service of others. The provisional character of politics does not act as a barrier to Christian action. We know that we are in transition from one order to another. All our life is limited by the knowledge that we work in faith and that the shape of the future is seen only 'through a glass darkly'. Limits are no threat to Christian freedom and the provisional character of political decision-making is not necessarily destructive of the Christian conscience. In this sense the various declarations on human rights together with the contemporary concern for the issue, may, despite their problematic language and thought-form, be seen as a useful and important political means of setting human limits to power and of protecting the life and worth of every citizen in society. Politics committed to such a concern for 'human rights' are always pursuing those provisional and limited solutions in the present which hold us to our aims and which achieve realistic and human goals in social relationships. Such political work requires a sympathetic participation by Christian people.

So in Christian social ethics there is both the given and the changing. The given is Jesus Christ, incarnate, crucified, risen and glorified, as the pattern for Christian life and work. The changing is the human social context. The Christian question concerns the significance of commitment to Jesus

Christ in the contemporary and changing social context. The contemporary context is the place in which we learn to grow towards the shape of life which is given in Jesus Christ. The practical politics of a love which is about serving and enabling life for others must be continually worked on and often fought for. They must not be culturally, philosophically or structurally fossilized. They must cope with change avoiding romanticism about the past, the baptism of the politics of the present and utopianism about the future. They must take seriously what Jesus said about the kingdom of God: 'Being asked by the Pharisees when the kingdom of God was coming, he answered them, "The kingdom of God is not coming with signs to be observed; nor will they say 'Lo here it is', or 'There', for behold the kingdom of God is in the midst of you." ' (Luke 17:20f.) Responses to particular issues should be viewed as examples of how Christians fulfil a responsible discipleship in the social order rather than as fixed and definitive answers which cannot be revised as understanding and circumstances change. Let us now briefly consider three examples.

Abortion

We have already commented on abortion earlier in this paper. In its own life the church approaches such decision-making in the context of the love of Jesus Christ which helps us to both give and receive. The struggle for individual rights — the rights of mother, child, father — must give way to a concern to make choices from the position of each in the terms of the needs of the others.

The mother must think of her decision in the light of the needs of the family and the sanctity of the life committed to her in conception. The father must think of the well-being of the mother and family. In such a context any decision for an abortion involves the whole community in a readiness to share in the cost of such a choice. The decision to give up life can never be taken out of self-interest or callously. Such a choice, in circumstances where, for example, the life of the mother is at risk, is always costly and needs the responsive love of others ready to support and to share.

In the wider community the attitude of the law must be determined by the way the community behaves. If the issue is seen in the terms of the struggle over rights, then law must take what steps it can to protect the weakest and most vulnerable people. An especial concern for the unborn child is an aspect of such concern.

Zimbabwe

The Christian community is present on either side of the struggle in Zimbabwe.[11] Its concern for the effect of the gospel upon the struggle may well assume different expressions according to the position Christians are in. Among the white community, for example, Christians need to witness to the creative possibilities for justice and peace in the yielding of power in the service of others. If, in the stubborn selfishness of power which refuses to take imaginative and effective action committed to justice for everyone, the judgement falls in the form of escalating violence and conflict, then Christians must have the courage to be the presence which speaks about judgement in political terms.

On the other side, as Christians identify with the struggle against the excesses of illegal and unconstitutional power and for a just and equal society in which race plays no political role, Christians need to both share in the suffering of a refugee people and enable those who fight to understand how chaos and violence threaten the future realization of their political aims. Christians must watch out for the opportunities for generosity which can help in creating peace without compromising justice.

The presence of Christians, whose fellowship is wider than the immediate context of the struggle and whose horizons should be further than the immediate choices, is in itself a witness against the adequacy of factionalism and a pointer to the new humanity of God's kingdom in Jesus Christ.

A Bill of Rights?

Our analysis of human rights and our commitment to a politics of hope and creative possibilities in the service of others encourages us to ask some searching questions about the present longing for a bill of rights.

Is this a 'Stop the world I want to get off' type of demand?

11. This comment antedated the settlement leading to independence in 1980.

Is this a guise for attempting to fossilize our constitutional arrangements against future development? It could be a dodge from engaging in political argument — a desire to have game, set and match before the first server has completed the first game. The strengths and weaknesses of fixed constitutional norms can be seen in places like the U.S.A. and India which have a written constitution guaranteed by the courts. Although the American tradition did eventually rescue the nation from the Nixon abuses, the fact of their happening and almost succeeding must make us cautious about how much can be achieved through trying to fix the system in a certain type of way. The best of fixed systems are more easily abused than sometimes we countenance.

It is one thing to enact a list of rights. It is quite another to see them put into practice. This is one of the problems with the various declarations on the subject. Declarations are good and laudable, but enforcement requires political will, choice and power. Christians are among those good at enunciating principles but not so good at wrestling with the actualities of power and seeing that things get done. Greater experience among us at this level would certainly underline the value of commitments to principles of justice. It would confront us with the central political realities of choice and with the challenge to give shape to the gospel at that point in social work.

The contemporary concern for human rights sets the context for much Christian witness in society today. We need to respond critically to the ideological roots of this concern and activity for people in a world where power is great and greatly abused. We need also to understand our own foundations in Jesus Christ, whose work achieved redemption and a new kingdom for the world. In this way, accepting our own limitations and working with a proper humility, we will seek, in identifying with the human concerns of those who work for rights, to bring the salt of the kingdom into a vital sphere of political life and work today. Above all else, such a Christian presence will share with any who endeavour to keep open the doors of hope in the face of the tyrants who desire to see them shut.

Reading List

J. N. D. Anderson, *Liberty, Law and Justice* (London, 1978).

D. Field, *Taking Sides: Ecology, Abortion, Divorce, Work, Race* (Leicester, 1975).

G. Forster, *Race and Responsibility* (Bramcote, Notts., 1965).

R. F. R. Gardner, *Abortion, the Personal Dilemma* (Exeter, 1972).

P. Sookhdeo (ed.), *All One in Christ?* (London, 1974).

J. H. Yoder, *The Politics of Jesus* (Grand Rapids, 1972).

R. Moore, 'Christianity and Human Rights', in *Christian Faith and Political Hopes*, ed. H. Willmer (London, 1979), pp. 47-64.

C. J. H. Wright, *Human Rights: A Study in Biblical Themes* (Bramcote, Notts., 1979).

Questions for Discussion

1   What are the strengths and weaknesses of saying that people do not have rights, but only responsibilities?

2   What is our assessment of the positions adopted by President Carter and the Soviet Union on human rights?

3   What is the political force for us of our commitment to Jesus Christ as the one who gave himself and his life in free obedient love for a broken and fallen world?

4   What has been missing from our evangelical thinking and experience to have made us so reticent about sharing in concern for human rights?

Epilogue
Tasks Which Await Us
John Stott

EPILOGUE

Tasks Which Await Us

I HAVE BEEN GREATLY ENCOURAGED BY THESE LAST FEW days. An evangelical conference on social ethics would have been impossible even ten years ago. It is good to see the growing number of comparatively young university and college lecturers in such fields as sociology, politics, economics and law, not to mention professional people, all of whom are Christians anxious to relate their faith to their academic discipline or professional life.

I have three suggestions to make about the further tasks which await us, and will conclude with the vision which, it seems to me, we should keep before us.

Answers

First, *we need to go beyond questions to answers,* however tentative our answers at first may be. The fact is that many more questions have been asked this week than answers given. Speaker after speaker has modestly declined to answer his own questions. It is not his field, he has said. Or he has not had time to develop his theme. Or he is a theologian *in via,* who would rather be a pilgrim than a heretic.

I am not criticizing this stance. There are several reasons why I agree with it. To begin with, it is the way of the scholar, who carefully weighs up all the evidence and cautiously balances the alternatives. Next, it is understandable because we are conscious of being novices in social ethics. We have much catching up to do. The backlog of work is enormous. Moreover, this attitude is welcome for its humility. If evangelical *enthusiasm* was 'a very horrid thing' to Bishop Butler, then evangelical *triumphalism* should seem horrid to us. Many of today's complex questions have no glib, easy or even sure answers. To concede this is humble because it is honest.

Nevertheless, we must not be content to remain for ever in a state of suspended animation. One of the best aimed of James Barr's poisoned arrows in his *Fundamentalism* is directed at our evangelical lack of theology. We have a stale tradition he suggests, not a fresh theology. 'Fundamentalism (from which he scarcely seems to distinguish evangelicalism) is a theologyless movement.' If we have a theology at all, he continues, it is either 'formalized' or 'fossilized'. This criticism is a broad generalization, as inaccurate as all generalizations are bound to be. Yet it contains an uncomfortable degree of truth. The resurgent evangelical movement has produced biblical scholars rather than creative thinkers.

What then shall we do? We must pray that God will raise up from our evangelical constituency creative, imaginative, courageous thinkers, in theology and ethics, in politics and economics, and in other fields of public life. They will need to be 'holistic' biblical thinkers, committed to the fourfold biblical scheme (of which we have been reminded) of creation, fall, redemption and consummation. They must also heed the warnings of Oliver O'Donovan and Howard Marshall against partial or selective positions, such as concentrate on the creation rather than the kingdom, on nature rather than history, on history rather than eschatology, or in each case vice versa. And they will need to be people who are prepared to explore, and to take the risks which all exploration demands, as they propose new ways of putting things and new ways of doing things which are strange to our evangelical tradition, though not alien to the biblical revelation.

If God answers our prayers for such pioneer thinkers, then it will be our responsibility to create the context within which they can do their work. The greatest peril to which any thinker is exposed is the isolation of his ivory tower. So we must not allow our thinkers to become isolated. For we need each other, men and women, thinkers and practitioners, tories and socialists, first-world and third-world citizens. We need each other not only in order to try out our ideas in a group which loves and trusts us, but also to allow the fellowship to check (not stifle) us, questioning us, where necessary challenging and correcting us, and always supporting and encouraging us. I visualize a developing community of evangelical thinkers, in the Shaftesbury Project and elsewhere, who are strongly committed to one another in biblical truth and steadfast love, and who with the confidence such fellowship brings are ready for perilous work on the frontier where the Christian mind and the secular mind engage with one another.

Actions

Secondly, *we need to go beyond words to actions.* This has been a conference on social ethics, rather than on social action, although to be sure participants have formed a healthy mix of academics and activists. And many are working productively, e.g. in the Nationwide Festival of Light and in the Evangelical Race Relations Group. Throughout the conference, however, there has lurked in the wings the shadowy spectre of Karl Marx, who was concerned, he said, not just (like the philosophers) to understand the world, but to change it. Repeatedly we have been reminded of his emphasis on *praxis*, of the need to integrate theory and practice, and of the new ways of 'doing theology' in Latin America which are inspired by the concrete challenges of socio-political reality.

But we Evangelicals tend to be strong in piety and weak in praxis. I remember hearing Dr. John Mackay, more than twenty years ago, while he was still President of Princeton Theological Seminary, say: 'Commitment without reflection is fanaticism in action; but reflection without commitment is the paralysis of all action.' All of us will agree that theological reflection is indispensable; I hope we agree that it is equally indispensable to translate our theology into action. Knowledge of Scripture can never be an end in itself. We are called not only to 'believe' the truth, but to 'do' or 'obey' it. As Bruce Nicholls has urged us, we must 'get involved'.

If we have another conference like this, and if the Shaftesbury Project study groups continue, I suggest that a self-conscious attempt be made to earth our thinking, *with a view to concrete action.* This might be something quite

modest like a single project in a local church such as a job
creation or retraining scheme, or it might be a more ambitious programme in terms of literary propaganda or
political agitation on some particular issue. But get involved
we must. As John put it centuries ago, 'My little children, let
us not love in word or talk, but in deed and in truth' (1 Jn.
3:18).

Passion

Thirdly, *we need to go beyond thought and action to passion.*
Our conference has certainly been more cerebral than
visceral. We have laughed a good deal, but we have not cried
very much. We have thought about, but I am not sure how
deeply we have felt, the tragedies and sufferings of the world.

I am certainly not advocating the artificial arousal of emo-
tion. But I am reminding you that the most influential leaders
in history, the social reformers and pioneers, have been men
and women of *action* because they have been men and
women of *thought* and *passion*.

The most powerful motivation in the public healing
ministry of Jesus was a combination of indignation and compassion. Confronted by the evils of disease and death he was
indignant. The verb *embrimaomai*, which is more than once
employed to indicate his response, was used of the 'snorting'
of horses, and so of humans snorting with anger or indignation (Mk. 1:43; Jn. 11:33, 38). But if the condition aroused
his indignation, the sufferer aroused his compassion (e.g.
Mk. 1:41).

Let me put this point in another way. An essential quality
of all leadership is vision. And vision combines a disenchant-
ment, even a disgust, with the *status quo* together with
dreams of what could be. Yes, we need evangelical dreamers
as well as evangelical thinkers, who will dream their dreams
of a better world, until their hearts burn within them and they
go out and do something.

Once or twice during the conference I have detected (and
been disturbed by) a note of pessimism. But pessimism is a
strange bedfellow for Christian faith.

The vision we need is the vision of God himself, the God of
the whole biblical revelation, the God of creation who made
all things fair and good, and made man male and female to
bear his image and subdue his world, the God of the covenant

of grace who in spite of human rebellion has been calling out
a people for himself, the God of compassion and justice who
hates oppression and loves the oppressed, the God of the
incarnation who made himself weak, small, limited and
vulnerable, and entered our pain and alienation, the God of
Resurrection, Ascension and Pentecost, and so of universal
authority and power, the God of the church or the kingdom
community to whom he has committed himself for ever, and
whom he sends into the world to live, serve, suffer and die,
the God of history who is working according to a plan and
towards a conclusion, the God of the *eschaton*, who one day
will make all things new.

There is no room for pessimism here, or for apathy either.
There is room only for worship, for expectant faith, and for
practical obedience in witness and service. For once we have
seen something of the glory of our God, and of the greatness
of his commission, we can only respond, 'I was not dis-
obedient to the heavenly vision.'

Indexes

BIBLICAL INDEX

GENERAL INDEX